The Crucifixion of Jesus

Roman crucifixions sought to degrade and dehumanise their victims in ways that destroyed their dignity and stigmatised their memory. Paul speaks of the cross as a 'scandal' or 'stumbling block', but the significance of this language has never been explored in terms of sexual violence. *The Crucifixion of Jesus* examines crucifixion as a form of torture, state terror, and sexual abuse. It reads recent accounts of torture alongside the presentation of crucifixion in the Passion narratives and other Greek and Roman sources.

Outlining compelling reasons for viewing Jesus as a victim of sexual abuse, it examines why this unsettling aspect of the narrative has remained 'hidden in plain sight' for so long, and what place it might have in discussions of rape culture past and present. It also asks whether other acts of sexual violence and rape might have happened during the mockery in the *praetorium*, or even on the cross itself. It argues that although the acknowledgement of this 'unspeakable violence' is deeply disturbing, breaking the silence can nonetheless have constructive consequences.

In addition to offering a more historical understanding of crucifixion, this book illuminates positive new aspects of resurrection, making it a probing read for scholars of biblical studies and for those interested in the interplay of religion and violence.

David Tombs is Howard Paterson Professor of Theology and Public Issues, and Director, Centre for Theology and Public Issues, at the University of Otago, New Zealand.

Rape Culture, Religion and the Bible
Series Editors:
Caroline Blyth
University of Auckland, New Zealand
Johanna Stiebert
University of Leeds, UK

Telling Terror in Judges 19
Rape and Reparation for the Levite's wife
Helen Paynter

Resisting Rape Culture
The Hebrew Bible and Hong Kong Sex Workers
Nancy Nan Hoon Tan

The Bible and Sexual Violence Against Men
Chris Greenough

Rape Culture, Purity Culture, and Coercive Control in Teen Girl Bibles
Caroline Blyth

Trafficking Hadassah
Collective Trauma, Cultural Memory, and Identity in the Book of Esther and in the African Diaspora
Ericka Shawndricka Dunbar

Vocation and Violence
The Church and #MeToo
Miryam Clough

Zeus Syndrome
A Very Short History of Religion-Based Masculine Domination
Joachim Kügler

The Crucifixion of Jesus
Torture, Sexual Abuse, and the Scandal of the Cross
David Tombs

For more information about this series, please visit: www.routledge.com/Rape-Culture-Religion-and-the-Bible/book-series/RCRB

The Crucifixion of Jesus
Torture, Sexual Abuse, and the Scandal of the Cross

David Tombs

LONDON AND NEW YORK

First published 2023
by Routledge
4 Park Square, Milton Park, Abingdon, Oxon OX14 4RN

and by Routledge
605 Third Avenue, New York, NY 10158

Routledge is an imprint of the Taylor & Francis Group, an informa business

© 2023 David Tombs

The right of David Tombs to be identified as author of this work has been asserted in accordance with sections 77 and 78 of the Copyright, Designs and Patents Act 1988.

The Open Access version of this book, available at www.taylorfrancis.com, has been made available under a Creative Commons Attribution 4.0 license.

Trademark notice: Product or corporate names may be trademarks or registered trademarks, and are used only for identification and explanation without intent to infringe.

British Library Cataloguing-in-Publication Data
A catalogue record for this book is available from the British Library

ISBN: 978-0-367-25765-1 (hbk)
ISBN: 978-1-032-43403-2 (pbk)
ISBN: 978-0-429-28975-0 (ebk)

DOI: 10.4324/9780429289750

Typeset in Times New Roman
by Apex CoVantage, LLC

Contents

Acknowledgements   vii

Introduction: A Salvadoran Execution   1

1   The Strippings   8
Introduction 8
Naked Prisoners at Abu Ghraib 8
Attitudes to Nudity in Roman Judaea 11
    Attitudes to Nudity in the Hebrew Bible 12
    Greek Attitudes to Nudity 13
    Roman Attitudes to Nudity 14
The Strippings of Jesus in the Praetorium 16
The Stripping at the Cross 17
Stripping, Enforced Nudity, and Sexual Abuse 21
Conclusion 24

2   The Mocking   27
Introduction 27
Sexualised Violence Against Male Detainees 28
Sexualised Violence Against Roman Captives 31
The Mocking of Jesus 34
    The Abuse of the Levite's Wife 36
    The Death of Herod Agrippa 38
Conclusion 39

3   Crucifixion   42
Introduction 42
The Stick 44
The Cross 44

From Assyrian Impalement to Roman Crucifixion 53
Roman Impalement? 57
Conclusion 62

4   Resurrection 66
Introduction 66
Blame and Stigma 69
A Bible Study on the Crucifixion of Jesus 71
Dignity and Recovery 72
Resurrection 75
Conclusion 78

Bibliography 81
Index 90

Acknowledgements

Too many people have assisted in the writing of this work to name each of them individually. But I am immensely grateful to colleagues, friends, family, and others who have both supported and challenged me over the years. My work has benefitted enormously from their interest, ideas, and generosity. I am especially grateful to Jayme Reaves, Rocío Figueroa, and Gerald West for recent collaborations on this research. My present institution, the University of Otago, and especially my colleagues in the Theology Programme, supported the research leave I enjoyed in 2022, which allowed the bulk of the writing to be completed. Colleagues in the School of Social and Cultural Studies at Victoria University Wellington offered a hospitable and quiet environment for this writing to happen. Earlier in the process, I was fortunate to participate in the residential workshop on religion and violence (2018) at the Centre of Theological Inquiry at Princeton. My fellow participants and the director, Will Storrar, encouraged and shaped my thoughts in many helpful ways. I have benefitted greatly in recent years from contact with other inspirational colleagues through the Shiloh Project, and I am especially grateful to Johanna Stiebert for her exceptionally valuable editorial suggestions on this book. The team at Routledge have been very patient and supportive since I first suggested contributing to the Focus Series. My partner, Rebecca Dudley, has been as positive and encouraging as ever and has gone far beyond what might reasonably be expected in terms of discussing the ideas and commenting on drafts. I am extremely grateful. A consequence of the help from different sources is that the book is much better than it would otherwise have been, but all views expressed are my own, and none of the people listed above is any way responsible for any failings that remain.

Scripture quotations are from the New Revised Standard Version Bible, copyright © 1989 National Council of the Churches of Christ in the United States of America. Used by permission. All rights reserved worldwide.

Unless otherwise noted, quotations from other ancient works are from the respective volume in the Loeb Classical Library, copyright Harvard University Press.

Introduction
A Salvadoran Execution

> Jesus . . . endured the cross, disregarding its shame.
>
> (Heb. 12:2)

This book offers a re-reading of crucifixion from the perspective of torture practices past and present. The Romans believed that pain and death could both be endured heroically. Some forms of execution therefore risked doing the opposite of what was intended. Instead of diminishing the condemned victim they risked transforming the condemned into a heroic martyr. Victims might redeem themselves in public memory by dying well. To prevent this, crucifixion was intended to be sickening and unspeakable, so degrading and overwhelming that a noble or heroic death for the victim was unthinkable. It was designed to not only end life but to disgrace the memory of the victim. It destroyed not only the man but also his reputation and standing as a man.[1] This made crucifixion a perfect penalty to demonstrate the death and disgrace that enslaved people, rebels, bandits, and anyone else who resisted Roman authority would face.

The sense of offence prompted Paul to refer to the cross as a 'scandal' or 'stumbling block' (1 Cor. 1:23). It is the *shame* of the cross rather than the *pain* of the cross that is recognised in Hebrews, which speaks of looking to Jesus who 'endured the cross, disregarding its shame, and has taken his seat at the right hand of the throne of God' (Heb. 12:2). The shame and scandal of the cross are quite often mentioned in contemporary Christian writing and Christian preaching. Yet to modern eyes, a traditional image of the crucifix is unlikely to be seen as deeply shameful, scandalous, or unspeakable. The pain of crucifixion is all too clear in these images, but the disgust and offensiveness associated with crucifixion in the first century are harder to understand.

From his arrest at Gethsemane until his death at Golgotha, Jesus was a political prisoner. Chapters 1–3 of this book show how the torture and mistreatment of political prisoners might offer a renewed understanding of the scandal of the cross which acknowledges the role of sexualised violence. To do this, the book draws on reports of prisoner abuse from recent times and from what can be discerned from the Greco-Roman world. With these sources in mind, the book turns to the

DOI: 10.4324/9780429289750-1

well-known passages in the gospels with an important question: what role did sexualised violence play in the stripping, mocking, and crucifixion of Jesus?

This has been a difficult book to write, and it will almost certainly be a difficult book to read. But the book is driven by the conviction that the biblical text matters. It is also shaped by the belief that recognising and confronting violence—especially sexual violence—matters. The book is therefore offered with the hope that a reading of Jesus' experience which is attentive to sexualised violence can contribute to better responses to sexual violence.

Using recent torture reports for a reading of first-century crucifixion may at first seem strange. To focus specifically on sexualised elements of torture may seem stranger still. As Natalie Wigg-Stevenson says: 'Like most Christians, perhaps, it never occurred to me that the torture Jesus experienced in the crucifixion could be interpreted as, have included or entailed or, even, be hermeneutically re-constituted as a form of sexual abuse' (Wigg Stevenson 2022, 668). The central claim of the book—that the violence to which Jesus was subjected should be properly named as sexualised violence—is offered with the awareness that this understanding is still unusual, and likely to be unsettling, despite the work which is increasingly published in this area. Part of the reason that it is disturbing to explore this claim is that sexual violence is often accompanied by shame, stigma, and silence. In many instances, sexual violence becomes, literally, 'unspeakable violence' (Tombs 2006). To write about crucifixion in this way is to open a conversation after a long silence. The book explores the twin dynamics of 'violence and silence' in the crucifixion story. It concludes with some implications of this argument for faith and practice in the church.

Academic writing invariably reflects personal interests and something of an author's biographical journey. It is appropriate for readers to ask how, and why, I have focussed on torture, sexualised violence, and crucifixion. For me, the challenge began with a question: how could the approaches advocated by Latin American liberation theologians offer new insights into crucifixion?

My interests in liberation theology go back to a chance discovery in an Oxford bookshop. In autumn 1985, I was starting my second year as an undergraduate student in philosophy and theology. I picked up the SCM 1981 edition of Gustavo Gutiérrez's book *A Theology of Liberation* in Blackwell's Bookshop. The cover showed two dramatic scenes which grabbed my attention. One scene showed a group of white-helmeted militarised police; the other showed the deprivation and poverty of a family in a Peruvian slum. The contrast was stark. I had spent the summer of 1985 travelling in Peru and had witnessed the inequalities of life there. The poverty and structural violence I had witnessed had not featured as topics during my first year reading theology and philosophy, but here was a book that put them centre stage on the front cover. Reading Gutiérrez's work changed my understanding of what theology is and why it matters (Tombs 1995, 2002a, 2015).

Trying to understand more about liberation theology re-orientated my studies as an undergraduate and led to a year of master's study at Union Theological Seminary in New York. The year at Union both cemented and broadened my interest in liberation theology. Courses with James Cone, Cornel West, Beverley Harrison, and Aloysius Pieris were each inspirational in their different ways. Above all, I remember the powerful classes with James Cone, and especially one piece of advice he offered those he taught. He told us that when we read theology, we should not just look at the questions that a theologian is addressing. We should also think about the questions that a theologian is not asking. He wanted students to be aware of the silences that shape theology, above all the silence of white scholars around black experience of injustice, racial oppression, and institutional violence (Cone 2018).

During my year at Union (1987–88) I was a member of the seminary's task force on Central America. I took a keen interest in church opposition to the US government support for right-wing military regimes in Central America (Smith 1996). In the summer of 1988, I travelled by bus from New York to Mexico, and then on to Guatemala, El Salvador, and Honduras. The recent history and current reality of poverty, inequality, and violence were very clear to see. In El Salvador, I visited a friend working for a church agency in an area heavily contested in the civil war. Throughout the country, the impact of the 12-year armed conflict (1980–91) was palpable: tensions about who might be spies, checks and searches of travellers on the busses, and one night, a firefight in the distance.

In 1993 I started a part-time PhD at Heythrop College, London. Heythrop was a Jesuit-founded theological college and provided an opportunity to explore liberation theology in El Salvador more deeply. I was particularly interested in Jon Sobrino's Christology and made further visits to El Salvador in the summers of 1996 and 1999 to learn more about Sobrino's work. The armed conflict had finished, but many of the underlying problems remained. Sobrino wrote on the 'crucified people' and insisted on the need for a response that takes the suffering of the cross seriously. Sobrino recognised crucifixion as a lived reality made present in the injustice and suffering of the context. He brought the crucifixion of Jesus into dialogue with the oppressed—and crucified—of El Salvador, and vice versa.

The subtitle of Sobrino's book, *The Principle of Mercy: Taking the Crucified People from the Cross*, captures the power of this distinctive outlook (Sobrino 1994). The mutual connections between the crucified people and the crucified Christ generate a demand for action. The Christian response to this demand should not be to gaze at the cross in either admiration or pity but to feel called to action.

For Sobrino, Jesus' crucifixion is a challenge: to recognise alongside Jesus those who are currently crucified, and to do everything possible to take them down from their crosses. As he puts it:

> We hope to establish, in this volume, that the sign of the times . . ., par excellence, is 'the existence of a crucified people'—in the words of Ignacio Ellacuría—and that the prime demand on us is that we 'take them down from the cross'.
>
> (Sobrino 1994, vii)

Back in London, following the 1996 visit, I read an account of an execution in El Salvador from 1983. This account led me to the work behind this book. It was the witness testimony, described by Salvadoran teenager Brenda Sánchez-Galan (Golden and McConnell 1986, 64–65; Smith 1996, 53). Sánchez-Galan had worked as an assistant in a medical centre for refugees near the capital San Salvador supported by the Lutheran Church. The military accused the medical centre of supporting political reforms and giving medical treatment to those opposed to the government. At one point, the military arrested the medical centre's Swiss doctor, tortured him, and detained him for six months. Eventually, he was released following pressure from the Swiss embassy. The security forces then targeted others at the medical centre. One night, soldiers abducted one of Sánchez-Galan's co-workers.[2] They tortured and raped her at the national guard headquarters. The next morning, the soldiers dragged her out into the public square. They made her bend over and a soldier shot her in a sexualised execution.

After the execution, Sánchez-Galan and her infant daughter sought refuge with the Lutheran Church, who helped them move to safety in Mexico City and then across the border to Texas. In 1984 she was one of the first Salvadoran refugees on a modern form of the 'underground railway' to be arrested in the United States. It was in Texas where she was able to tell her story to those who helped her. She repeated it in her testimony in court.

By the time I read the story in the 1990s, sexual violence during armed conflict had started to receive much greater international media attention than it had been given in 1983. The use of sexual violence in the 'ethnic cleansing' in Bosnia (1992–95) and genocide in Rwanda (1994) had shown quite clearly that sexual violence during conflict is not just an individual crime. Rather, it has a political dimension that requires more systemic analysis. Reading the story told by Sánchez-Galan brought home the role of sexual violence in the Salvadoran conflict. Liberation theologians, whom I greatly admired, had written such powerful works on the violence against the poor. Yet for some reason very little attention had been given to sexual violence. Jon Sobrino offered extraordinary insight into the cross and 'crucified people' of El Salvador, yet his work said little on sexual violence in torture and nothing explicit about sexual violence and the cross.

The Sánchez-Galan testimony prompted me to take a detour in my Christological research. I started to investigate the issue of sexual violence in the Salvadoran conflict in more depth. I hoped to understand what lay behind such an act of sexualised violence and also why it did not receive more attention in theological works. How were those who suffered sexualised violence to be helped down from the cross? How was this possible if the form of crucifixion they experienced was never spoken about? What I expected to be a relatively short detour into an important but brief side issue became a long-term interest. Eventually, 'unspeakable violence' became the primary focal point for my PhD on crucifixion (Tombs 2004). To understand what was behind the violence, and the silence which surrounded it, I was drawn into reading torture reports and truth commission publications documenting a wide range of prisoner abuses in detention during military dictatorships and repressive regimes in Brazil, Chile, Uruguay, Argentina, El Salvador, and Guatemala during the 1970s and 1980s.[3] It was disturbing reading. An evocative title for an Amnesty International collection on worldwide torture reports from that time is *A Glimpse of Hell* (Forrest 1996). Reading these reports might be described as an education in 'the classrooms of hell'.[4]

My first opportunity to present on the new direction in my work was at the Society of Biblical Literature International Meeting in Kraków in 1998. I had submitted a proposal for a paper on the interpretive principles of liberationist hermeneutics in Latin America. However, I decided instead to offer a reading of crucifixion influenced by liberationist biblical hermeneutics, specifically by contextual awareness of Latin American state terror and torture practices. The paper was published the following year in *Union Seminary Quarterly Review* (Tombs 1999, 2018).[5]

The article argued that Roman approaches to crucifixion could be better understood in light of two insights from the study of torture under authoritarian regimes in Latin America. First, crucifixions as public punishments should be understood as spectacles of 'state terror'; that is, they serve a political purpose of social intimidation. They are not just punishments against an individual but hold a message for anyone who might oppose Rome. Second, the prevalence of nudity and sexual violence in torture suggests that a sexual dimension is not an incidental detail in torture but an integral element of the terror. The article then examines how both of these insights might help towards a reading of Roman crucifixions.

First, there is clear and explicit biblical evidence for the repeated stripping and exposure of Jesus before a whole cohort of soldiers in the *praetorium*. This is followed by naked exposure before the crowd at crucifixion. This punitive stripping and forced nudity deserve to be recognised as sexual humiliation, which constitutes sexual abuse.

Second, in addition to naming Jesus as a victim of sexual abuse on account of the stripping, the article considered the possibility that Jesus may have experienced rape or sexual assault, which is not recorded in the text. To be clear: this is not explicitly attested in the text, and no firm conclusion is possible. Nonetheless, the possibility of further assault should be acknowledged. The question deserves to be asked, even if it cannot be answered with certainty.

This book revisits the article and draws on subsequent work in my PhD, and other work since then, on the questions it raises. Chapters 1–3 will follow the narrative sequence and focus successively on the stripping, the mocking, and the crucifixion.

Chapter 1 will address the repeated strippings in the *praetorium* and the naked exposure on the cross as forms of sexualised violence which are common in torture. Stripping and enforced nudity are appropriate starting points for investigating Jesus' experience of sexualised violence both because they come first in the narrative and because they are clearly and explicitly attested in the gospels. This chapter argues that the stripping and nudity offer compelling evidence for Jesus to be acknowledged as a victim of sexualised violence and therefore a victim of sexual abuse. This is not just an acknowledgement of how the stripping should be understood in today's terms but also an appropriate way to see its significance at the time.

Chapter 2 asks whether Jesus might have been subjected to further sexual assault in the *praetorium* as part of the mocking. Might the 'mocking' of Jesus have included more than the gospel texts disclose? It is unlikely that there will ever be a definitive answer. However, the chapter will suggest that reading the biblical text alongside both recent and ancient torture accounts raises disturbing questions. The disturbing account in Josephus of soldiers mocking statues of the daughters of Herod Agrippa after his death in 44 CE suggests questions for the mockery of Jesus as King of the Jews in c. 33 CE.

Chapter 3 turns to the cross itself. It returns to a particularly confronting element which was mentioned in passing but not developed at length in my earlier work (Tombs 1999). The first-century Roman philosopher Seneca the Younger mentions that some crucifixions could involve the extreme sexual violence of genital impalement. How are Seneca's words to be understood? What might such crucifixions involve? This chapter investigates how crucifixion might be viewed in relation to impalement and whether crucifixion could have included penetrative sexualised violence. It suggests that more work is needed on this question.

The material in Chapters 1–3 is challenging and in many ways repugnant. This is hard to avoid when recounting events that by their nature are intended to dehumanise and degrade the victim and terrorise and sicken those who witness them. It is not the purpose of this research to shock or distress readers, but the sequence of chapters in an attentive journey to the cross is inevitably shocking and distressing. Stripping, mocking, and crucifixion narrate something of a staged 'descent' into the depravity of torture, including sexualised violence. The progression of violence addressed in Chapters 1–3 might be one way to view the Christian confession that Christ 'descended into hell'.[6]

The questions I had about what liberation theology might offer that started for me that day in Blackwell's Bookshop in 1985—and which later led me to reflecting on 'unspeakable violence'—have unfortunately continued to be relevant, even urgent. Recent years have been marked by further revelations of sexual violence against detainees and torture victims. The scandals of US forces at Abu Ghraib in Iraq (2003–04) and ongoing torture reports from many other countries (e.g., Sri Lanka, Syria, Libya, South Sudan, Ukraine) have underlined that sexualised violence in torture is a global phenomenon.

This work has led to reflection on painful and difficult testimonies, often at first hand, of torture, both in Roman times and up to the present day. Over the years, I have had the opportunity to work with many groups of Christians in Bible study and reflection, as well as work through these issues with colleagues at academic conferences. People sometimes ask, 'what positive purpose is served by this research?' or 'what is gained by investigating the "way of the cross"?' Chapter 4 offers a brief response to these important questions by focussing on victim-blaming, stigma, and the recovery of dignity.

If we understand crucifixion differently, we may also discover new insights into the Christian understanding of resurrection. In this reading, resurrection is not just the physical restoration of the body, but it also affirms the restoration of dignity as God's embodied response to crucifixion and all that crucifixion involved. The Christian tradition affirms the importance of seeking and telling the truth, even truths which might be painful, disturbing and in some ways 'unspeakable'. In fact, the Christian tradition affirms that truth can be liberating and set us free. This is not an easy path, but it can be explored with a reassurance that nothing that a person might be forced to endure can separate that person from the love of God (Rom. 8.35–39).

I believe that a key challenge to Christian faith is to acknowledge the cross and speak of salvation *despite* the cross. Over the centuries, much has been said about finding salvation in the cross, or through the cross. I follow Sobrino's lead here: the proper task for Christians is not to glorify or romanticise the suffering of the cross but to resist the cross and find ways to take victims down from cross. A guide for Chapter 4 is therefore how the understanding of the cross in Chapters 1–3 might help bring others down from the cross. Thus, whilst Chapters 1–3 address one scandal of the cross by focussing on the scandalous violence Jesus experienced, Chapter 4 addresses a very different scandal of the cross. It looks at how resurrection might be seen in the shadow of the cross, and how human dignity might be recovered and restored despite the horror of the cross.

Notes

1 Because the focus on the book is on crucifixion as a form of sexualised violence against male victims—and against Jesus of Nazareth in particular—I will usually refer to victims of crucifixion as men. There is evidence that women were crucified as well as men, but explicit reference to women being crucified are very rare. The clearest is Josephus' account of a freedwoman named Ide who was crucified in the time of Tiberias (*Antiquities*, 18.80). Other writings suggest that women were included in mass crucifixions but give little detail. For example, Tacitus reports that at the time of Pedanius Secundus, the ancient tradition of crucifying all slaves in the household was upheld despite the protests of the people (*Annals*, 14:45). Although the word 'punishment' (*supplicium*) is used in this passage—rather than the word 'cross' (*crux*)—it is reasonable to understand punishment as 'slaves' punishment' (*supplicium servile*), which was a euphemistic reference to crucifixion. If this was the usual practice then presumably women and children were also crucified in other cases as well, even though sources do not usually report this.
2 Regrettably the name of the executed health worker is not preserved in these accounts.
3 On using torture reports in theology and biblical studies, see Cavanaugh (1998), Neafsey (2014), Aguilar (2015) and Menéndez-Antuna (2022).
4 The phrase 'classrooms of hell' was used on social media in a polemical way to condemn the theological education I supposedly must have received to write of Jesus as a victim of sexual abuse. Although the comment was intended to be dismissive, in some ways it captured an important truth about the research.
5 The article was reprinted in 2018 with a retrospective response and reflection from Fernando Segovia, who had been a co-chair of the session (with Jeremy Punt) when the paper was first presented. See Tombs (2018) and Segovia (2018).
6 Forrest (1996).

1 The Strippings

'They stripped him.'

(Matt. 27:28)

Introduction

This chapter draws on torture reports and political prisoner documentation to discuss the stripping of Jesus. It provides an overview of how stripping and enforced nudity can be used in detention centres to humiliate prisoners, with particular attention to the mistreatment of Iraqi prisoners at Abu Ghraib (2003–04). Attitudes towards nudity in Roman Judaea are analysed. The chapter also examines the strippings in the *praetorium* and then turns to the stripping and enforced nudity on the cross. Finally, the chapter discusses why the stripping of Jesus should be named as sexualised violence and a form of sexual abuse.

Naked Prisoners at Abu Ghraib

Following the approach advocated in liberation theology, the reading of Jesus' stripping that is offered in this chapter will be a contextual reading (Tombs 1995). It follows an initial analysis of the lived experience of stripping and enforced nudity endured by torture victims in more recent times. This is to develop a clearer sense of the significance and impact of stripping and nudity in the present, in order to notice its use and think more seriously about its purpose in the past. To do this, I turn especially to the mistreatment of prisoners at Abu Ghraib in Iraq by US military police (MP).[1]

On arrival at Abu Ghraib, prisoners were stripped and searched. This initial stripping at a detention facility can serve a legitimate security purpose, to identify anything detainees might use as a weapon. However, it also signals an important transition for prisoners. From this point, they are stripped of autonomy and under the complete control of the guards. The stripping formalises this change and makes clear the power of the guards in contrast to the powerlessness of the prisoner.

Once inside the facility, stripping can subsequently be used to repeatedly remind prisoners of their new position. Stripping and enforced nudity in detention were

DOI: 10.4324/9780429289750-2

often used at Abu Ghraib without any security justification. It is sufficient that these enact a relationship of abusive control and embarrass and humiliate a detainee.

Clothing is more than a physical covering; it also has psychological and social significance. It helps someone to know and to express who they are, and to communicate their standing in relation to others. Repeated stripping and periods of enforced nudity during detention may appear relatively minor forms of mistreatment. But the psychological impact is more potent than first appears. The power to strip becomes an effective way to undermine a prisoner's sense of both physical safety and psychological security. In terms of physical safety, nakedness heightens the threat of violence and increases the sense of physical vulnerability. In terms of secure psychological identity and social standing, the forcible stripping of clothing is connected with the stripping of dignity and self-confidence. Stripping and nakedness can therefore be used to erode a prisoner's sense of self and of who they are as a human being and as an individual. It can also be a first step to different forms of other sexualised violence during torture.

Photos taken at Abu Ghraib in October-November 2003 were reported by a whistle-blower in the military in January 2004, and publicised by the media in April 2004. One of the most searing images, from 5 November 2003, shows a figure standing on a crate with electrical wires attached to his fingers. His body is covered by a dark loose sack-type garment, and his head is hooded by another sack. He stands with his arms outstretched in a manner that is suggestive of a crucifixion pose. In another notorious photo, a naked prisoner is shown crawling out of his cell. He is tethered by a leash around his neck, and the leash is held by a female guard, subsequently identified as MP Lynndie England. In other photos, prisoners are standing handcuffed against railings and bars. Some are struggling to support themselves and are slumped in uncomfortable positions as if they have been left to stand like this for a considerable period.

Whilst each of these images is acutely disturbing in its own way, one feature characteristic of many of the photos is nudity. In some photos the prisoners are either entirely naked, or they are wearing only a hood, or some covering on their head, while their bodies are fully exposed. The International Committee of the Red Cross visited Abu Ghraib in October 2003. It reported that abuses against detainees included 'the practice of keeping [prisoners] completely naked in totally empty concrete cells and in total darkness' and parading prisoners naked in front of guards and other prisoners (Danner 2004, 6). When questioned about this, the military authorities explained that this practice was 'part of the process' (Danner 2004, 6–7).

Prisoners experienced the stripping as an intense violation. One prisoner, Hayder Sabbar Adb who features in the photos (prisoner 13077), describes his protest when he was ordered to strip:

> Then the interpreter told us to strip. . . . We told him 'You are Egyptian and a Muslim we can't do that'. When we refused to take off our clothes, they beat us and tore our clothes off with a blade.
>
> (Danner 2004, 3–4)[2]

For many prisoners being stripped was a repeated and routine mistreatment. Interrogators at the prison directed the night-shift guards to prepare a prisoner for interrogation and 'Make sure he has a bad night' (Danner 2004, 9). A 'bad night might involve physical beating and further stripping and hooding to intimidate and humiliate the prisoner. To add further humiliation, the prison had a large box of pink women's panties which were sometimes used as make-shift hoods on male prisoners. The male prisoners were especially embarrassed when female guards witnessed their nakedness or participated in other abuses related to their nudity.

The Bush administration claimed that the abuses at Abu Ghraib were unauthorised and denounced the perpetrators as 'bad apples' and rogue operators. However, multiple reports support the view that the stripping of prisoners at Abu Ghraib was a routine part of the interrogation process. It was 'standard operating procedure' in what was euphemistically described as 'enhanced interrogation'. Further disclosures of abuses at Guantanamo, and Bagram airbase in Afghanistan, as well as concerns over special 'renditions' of prisoners for aggressive interrogation in the post-9/11 era of a so-called Global War on Terror suggest that sexual humiliation through stripping was widespread (Begg 2006, 191).

In 1994 the United States ratified the UN Convention Against Torture: officially, torture is not, and cannot be, condoned, justified, excused, or sanctioned. Along with the Geneva Conventions, this UN treaty should have provided detainees with solid protection against cruel treatment. The Bush administration paid lip-service to the conventions in principle, and insisted that torture is wrong. Yet in practice US policy undermined the Convention Against Torture and the Geneva Conventions by justifying and endorsing harsh interrogation procedures. Furthermore, one of the ways that the United States sought to get around the prohibition against torture was to approve practices which put less emphasis on direct violence and drew more on humiliation, sensory deprivation, and self-inflicted pain, rather than on directly inflicted physical violence.

Sensory deprivation at Abu Ghraib frequently involved temporary blinding, which helps to explain why hooding was so common. Stress positions were also widely practised at Abu Ghraib. Stress positions were a means to inflict severe physical pain over a prolonged period whilst avoiding obvious physical marks. Prisoners were forced to stand for hours, hand-cuffed to railings, and often with arms outstretched. Stress positions offer a level of deniability because they do not leave contact marks and if included in records can be described in understated ways. The pretence that this is not torture or cruelty or inhumane treatment could only be maintained by ignoring the enormous gap in power between prisoner and guard, alongside the fact that a guard could force a prisoner to maintain the stress position long beyond the point when it became unbearable.

Even so, the pretence was a useful device, especially because of a legal ruling by the European Court (Ireland v UK, 1978) in relation to Northern Ireland. The judgement in this case set a legal precedent for torture, inhuman treatment, and degrading treatment, and drew a distinction between, on the one hand, some use of stress positions and, on the other, torture. The judgment did not suggest that *all* stress positions constituted acceptable practice, or were legally permissible, but it offered an opportunity for the US administration to argue that stress positions could be distinguished from torture. This could then be used to claim that the administration upheld the prohibition against torture while permitting 'acceptable' stress positions.

The distinction the US administration tried to sustain between infliction of stress positions vs torture is also relevant to enforced nudity, because stripping and enforced nudity are effective means to another form of pain. Just as stress positions lead to physical pain, stripping and enforced nudity lead to psychological pain (Sands 2004). Stripping was used intentionally at Abu Ghraib as a psychological weapon and was experienced as profound trauma.

The shame-filled consequences of forced stripping are more destructive than any short-lived embarrassment; they can be both powerful and long-lasting. When there is a public audience, the shame associated with involuntary nudity is heightened further. This is compounded further when the nudity is captured in photos and videos in ways that allow the shame to be displayed and circulated more widely. The intended purpose of taking the videos and photos at Abu Ghraib has been contested. The MP Sabrina Harman claims that photos were a way for her to show what really happened if she ever needed to answer for abuses. Others have suggested that the photos were used to exert additional pressure on prisoners, since prisoners were told that the photos would be released more widely if they were not compliant, and even that the photos would be sent to family members. At any rate, the prisoners had no agency to resist, no control over the exposure or display of their nakedness, and no protection against intense shaming.

In addition to shame, stripping and nudity also created a heightened sense of vulnerability and exposed detainees to other mistreatments. One of the Abu Ghraib photos shows a naked prisoner trying to shrink away from a snarling dog. Again, he is more vulnerable than a clothed prisoner would be, as he has been deprived of a protective layer of clothing, but also because he is weakened on account of humiliation at a psychological level. In other cases, the exposure of genitals was escalated to other abuses; this will be discussed in Chapter 3.

Attitudes to Nudity in Roman Judaea

Stripping and enforced nudity carried a powerful gendered significance in the first century, just as they do today. Social attitudes varied on some aspects of nudity depending on cultural beliefs and values. However, in the first-century Roman Empire, and especially in the Roman province of Judaea, forcibly stripping a man and displaying him naked in public was readily understood as indicative of conquest and defeat, as profoundly shaming of the humiliated victim, and, in Jewish eyes, as an especially offensive punishment.

Attitudes to Nudity in the Hebrew Bible

The Hebrew Bible strongly censures public nudity as shameful (Vogelzang and van Bekkum 1986, 272).[3] Mark Finney (2013, 127) points out that:

> The male genitalia were frequently denoted by the euphemism 'shame' (in such phrases as 'he covered his shame', Jubilees 3:27, 30; cf. Isa 58:7; Ezek 16:22, 35–39; Job 26:6), and Paul, too, spoke of the 'shameful' parts of the body, meaning the sexual organs (1 Cor. 12:23).

The association of public nudity and shame is particularly clear in Genesis 2–3. Initially, Adam and Eve are naked but not ashamed (Gen. 2:25). However, because they heed the serpent and eat from the Tree of Knowledge, they become aware they are naked and make loincloths for themselves (Gen. 3:6–7).

The story of Noah in Genesis 9:20–27 also conveys the strength of feeling around genital exposure. After the flood Noah plants a vineyard, and when the harvest comes he drinks the wine. In his drunken state he lies uncovered in his tent and falls asleep. His son Ham 'saw the nakedness of his Father' and told his brothers Shem and Japheth. Shem and Japheth then take a garment and enter the tent with their eyes averted to cover Noah's nakedness. When Noah awakes and realises what Ham 'had done to him', he blesses Shem and Japheth and curses Ham's son Canaan. Because Noah's response is so fierce—and because sexual activity is often referenced euphemistically in the Bible—there are different interpretations offered on the nature of Ham's offense and to explain Noah's reaction. The offences Ham has been accused of committing range from voyeurism, to castration or paternal incest, to possible maternal incest (Bergsma and Hahn 2005).[4] Even if the most literal interpretation is assumed—that Ham did no more than look upon his father naked—the story underlines the sense of taboo and stigma in naked exposure. A less literal reading of Ham seeing Noah's nakedness is that Ham committed a more physical form of sexual impropriety. In this reading, the passage provides an important example of how a narrative might use the convention of exposing and beholding nakedness to signify a more physical act of sexual violence. Those who take this view point to the language used, especially that Noah realises what Ham 'had done to him'. In support of this, the phrase 'to uncover nakedness' is used in other biblical contexts for depraved sexual relations.

Close connections between conquest, captivity, and the shame of forced nudity are clear in a number of passages in the Hebrew Bible. Lamentations uses the 'shame' of nakedness to speak figuratively of the fall of Jerusalem and the city's disgrace: 'Jerusalem sinned grievously so she has become a mockery; all who honoured her despise her, for they have seen her nakedness; she herself groans, and turns her face away' (Lam. 1:8). A similar warning is given to Babylon: 'Your nakedness shall be uncovered, and your shame shall be seen. I will take vengeance, and I will spare no one' (Isa. 47:3). Likewise, a warning to Nineveh: 'I am against you, says the Lord of hosts, and will lift up your skirts over your face; and I will let nations look on your nakedness, and kingdoms on your shame' (Nah. 3:5).

There are also references to the practice of exposing male prisoners to public shame and ridicule. In Isaiah, the prophet warns that 'so shall the king of Assyria lead away the Egyptians as captives and Ethiopians as exiles, both the young and the old, naked and barefoot with buttocks uncovered, to the shame of Egypt' (Isa. 20:4). For the Jews, this is an omen of what they too can expect from the Assyrians.[5] Likewise, 2 Samuel 10:4–5 describes David's envoys being seized by the Ammonite King Hanun and sent back with their beards half shaved and their garments cut off 'in the middle at their hips'. Jewish disapproval of public nudity and the association between nakedness and shame would have deepened the sense of humiliation associated with forced nudity following military conquest.

Greek Attitudes to Nudity

Although less directly relevant to crucifixion in first-century Roman Judaea than Jewish attitudes to nudity, it is useful to note that Greek culture had more mixed attitudes to nudity than is sometimes assumed. In some contexts, public nudity was celebrated. There was a tradition of artistic depictions of divine and mythic figures as nude and heroic. Greek statues show both male and female figures as naked and beautiful. However, in day-to-day life attitudes to the naked body were more complicated. Displays of nudity were governed and circumscribed by convention and only socially appropriate in certain specific contexts. In contests, athletes' nudity was acceptable and even celebrated. Hence, the word 'gymnasium' is derived from the word *gymnos* ('naked' or 'nude').[6] Likewise, nudity appears to have been common at 'symposia' where men met to talk, drink, and be entertained.[7] However, the conventions of the gymnasium and the symposium were exceptions rather than norms. It would be a mistake to take them as evidence that Greek culture embraced nudity in all, or even many, situations. The gymnasium and symposium were prestige social settings in which nudity functioned as a display of high social status. In these contexts, the more usual social expectations and sanctions could be set aside. By contrast, in their everyday affairs, the Greeks maintained much stricter expectations around clothing. Clothing also conveyed status and identity, and respectable people were not naked in public. Nudity in public was generally associated with ignominy, with the disreputable not the respectable.

To understand the social meaning of nudity, it is also important to recognise the difference between choosing to be naked in certain appropriate social settings—in which one enjoys social privileges and has control over oneself—versus being forcibly stripped and exposed naked in a hostile social setting, especially if one is vulnerable to further violence in such a state. The Greeks did not see nudity as inherently shameful, yet not all displays of the naked body were acceptable. Specifically, for the Greeks, the ancient sources attest that the stripping and forcible exposure of an enemy were forms of profound insult and created opportunities for even greater humiliation.

Stripping the armour of a conquered enemy in warfare reflects the material value of armour but also carries a high symbolic value. Stripping demonstrates that the enemy is now powerless and vulnerable. Homer's *Iliad* conveys the emotional horror associated with the stripping of a fallen warrior. The *Iliad* gives detailed accounts of the deaths of Patroclus and Hector. The emotional intensity and sense of outrage around stripping the bodies of Patroclus and Hector are as heightened as those reserved for their actual deaths. In the case of Patroclus, Hector is 'most eager' to cut off the head of Patroclus and to fix it on a pole set in the wall (*Iliad*, 18.172–177). However, the Greeks fight fiercely to prevent this and retrieve his body. They eventually recover the body of Patroclus so that it can be burnt with dignity. In the case of Hector, the body is captured, and stripped, and dragged in disgrace around the walls of the city over many days. Hector's father, King Priam, eventually begs Achilles to end the sustained public humiliation of his son's corpse. Achilles, reminded of his own father, agrees that the body can be returned for an honourable funeral.

It is the humiliation of the body rather than the value of the armour that gives emotional intensity to the scenes in the *Iliad*. The stripping of armour serves as form of humiliation and makes the victim vulnerable to further sexualised humiliation.

Roman Attitudes to Nudity

The Romans were generally more conservative around matters of nudity than the Greeks. For Roman men, there was no problem in being naked in one's home in front of slaves. Romans also appear to have considered it appropriate to be naked amongst one's social peers at the public baths or at the gymnasium (Jensen 2012, 298–300). Yet, the baths and the gymnasium were once more exceptions rather than the norm. More conversative voices even expressed concerns over where the acceptability of nudity at the baths and gymnasia might lead, and saw these settings as encouraging shameless behaviour. Therefore, even when men were at the baths and the gymnasia there was still an expectation of decorum and restraint rather than of ostentatious display.

A Roman citizen was mindful of how they were viewed by others, and especially by others of their social standing or above. They were careful to avoid any indication that their appearance or behaviour suggested someone of lower standing. Outside the baths and the gymnasia, nudity was likely to be associated with enslaved people, sex workers, and those of ill repute and little honour, and so was to be avoided by respectable citizens.

Only Roman adult men qualified as citizens and there was, consequently, strong association between citizenship and masculinity. Enacting masculinity—or manliness—was important not only for a man's personal reputation but for the good standing and honour of Roman citizenship as a whole. To be seen naked in public was a serious breach of respectable manly behaviour and would have been very damaging to the reputation as both man and citizen.

A citizen who went naked did not just compromise their own reputation but brought disrepute by association upon the manliness of all respectable Roman citizens. For a Roman citizen to be stripped naked by someone else was an insult not just to the individual but to all Romans. This gave Roman clothing a more political significance than might at first be obvious. Craig Williams argues that the Romans' understanding of manliness was all-important in the Roman world (Williams 2010). The most important attribute of this masculinity was that a Roman man exercised control and autonomy over himself and his body, as well as control and autonomy over his family and slaves and their bodies.

The significance of this association between manliness, control, and bodily autonomy can be seen most clearly in Roman attitudes to sexuality and sexual activities. A Roman man who cared for his reputation was expected always to take the role of the insertive/penetrative partner and never the penetrated partner in sexual activities. The terms 'heterosexual' and 'homosexual' do not fit easily with the Roman outlook, at least in terms of suggesting an underlying fixed sexual orientation. If he chose, a Roman man could have sexual relations with male or female slaves, or male or female prostitutes, or non-Roman women, men, girls, or boys, without fear of disapproval or criticism of being unmanly. In other words, a Roman man was at liberty to have sexual relations with a wide range of people recognised as his social inferiors. However, these sexual relations were only socially acceptable if he was in the role of penetrator; he could not allow himself to be penetrated and maintain his honour as a Roman citizen. Taking the role of penetrator versus penetrated was not a matter of personal choice or preference but a social convention backed by strong social disapproval. Penetrating was seen as manly, whereas being penetrated was the role appropriate to a social inferior.[8] The stigma against a Roman man being penetrated was so profound that Roman men were expected to refrain from (or at least not be caught in) any sexual relations with other Roman men. Taking the penetrative role with another Roman man was unacceptable, because it created a situation in which the other Roman man was penetrated; and this brought shame on all Roman men. Likewise, a Roman man was expected to avoid sexual relations with freeborn Roman women, apart from his own wife, so as not to harm the reputation of the wife or daughter of another Roman citizen.

The Romans made much of their social superiority as civilised Romans as opposed to foreign barbarians. To strip a foreign prisoner publicly, regardless of whether the prisoner is male or female, is to demonstrate power and control over the prisoner. This power is often gendered and constructed as manly. By contrast, in being stripped, a prisoner is displayed as powerless, and a stripped male prisoner is shown to be unmanly. Stripping prisoners to humiliate them, and publicly exposing a prisoner to shame them further, would not have seemed strange.

Stripping captives in this way communicates a similarly gendered message of power for the Romans as it did to the guards at Abu Ghraib. Furthermore, for a Jewish man to be stripped and exposed by the Romans would probably have been especially disturbing for two reasons. First, as noted above, Jewish views on nudity were especially strongly associated with shame, and tradition typically proscribed any form of public nudity. Second, if the stripping involved full nudity, it would have involved exposure of the circumcised penis. One of the prejudices shown in Roman writings towards the Jews is their derogatory view of circumcision. Circumcision was regarded as genital mutilation and sometimes taken to suggest that Jewish men were always in a state of sexual arousal. Exposing the circumcised penis would have been an easy target for sexual insult and for mockery of either the manliness or the sexual restraint and decorum of the one who was stripped, while conferring power and superiority on those who did the stripping.

The Strippings of Jesus in the *Praetorium*

Each of the gospel accounts of the mockery and crucifixion of Jesus has its own distinctive concerns. Michael Trainor offers a careful examination of each account in his book *The Body of Jesus and Sexual Abuse* (Trainor 2014). As Trainor argues, taken together these show a high level of sexual humiliation in the way that Jesus was stripped, insulted, and eventually crucified. Chris Greenough offers a similar assessment of the stripping in the chapter 'Jesus Too?' in his recent book (Greenough 2021, 62–86). The stripping is also the central concern in the edited collection by Reaves et al. (2021).[9]

To examine the stripping in more detail, this section will look at the stripping in the *praetorium* (the governor's palace) and then at the cross, with particular focus on Mark 15:15–20 and Matthew 27:26–31. It draws especially on work by biblical scholar Gerald West (2021). The next section will then turn to the stripping and naked exposure on the cross, especially in John.

Mark 15:15, Matthew 27:26, and John 19:1 each mention that Jesus was flogged. Mark and Matthew have the flogging at the end of the trial (John has the flogging midway through the trial), and both report that after the flogging Jesus is handed over to the Roman soldiers to mock him inside the *praetorium*. Although none of these accounts is explicit as to whether Jesus was stripped for the purpose of flogging, and although Luke's account does not mention a flogging at all, there is good reason to think that before Jesus was flogged he was stripped of his clothing because the common convention for flogging is that the victim be naked, or at least near-naked.[10]

In Mark and Matthew, once inside the *praetorium*, the soldiers are assembled, and the mockery begins. Mark describes Jesus as being dressed in purple. There is no mention in Mark of needing to strip Jesus before dressing him. So, either Jesus was brought into the *praetorium* already unclothed, or he was re-dressed after the flogging and then stripped again before being clothed in purple (Mark 15:17). Because Mark does not explicitly mention whether Jesus was brought naked into the *praetorium* or was stripped on arrival, it is easy to assume that the mention of stripping Jesus in Mark 15:20 is the first and only time he was stripped as part of the flogging and mockery. This is incorrect. The stripping in Mark 15:20 must be at least the second stripping (if Jesus was brought into the *praetorium* naked at v. 15), or possibly the third stripping (if he was reclothed after the flogging at v. 15, and therefore needed to be stripped again to be dressed in purple at v. 17). The reference to '[they] put his own clothes on him' (Mark 15:20) shows that when the soldiers dressed Jesus in purple, he was either already naked from the flogging, or they had stripped him of his own clothes (*himatia* is plural) before putting the purple on him.

Matthew is probably familiar with Mark's account but makes some important changes which bring the repeated strippings into even clearer focus (West 2021, 120–122). Like Mark, Matthew refers to the flogging as taking place immediately before Jesus is brought into the *praetorium* (Matt. 27:26–27). Matthew also makes explicit that Jesus was stripped when he first arrived in the *praetorium* (Matt. 27:28). Jesus is then dressed in a scarlet robe. Following the mockery, the soldiers strip Jesus again (Matt. 27:31). This sequence suggests that Jesus was stripped first for the flogging, and then reclothed (presumably in his own clothes) to be brought into the *praetorium*. He was then stripped a second time and dressed in the scarlet robe. He was then stripped a third time, and his own clothes put back on him. As in Mark 15:20, in Matthew 27:31 the word used for Jesus' own clothes is *himatia* (plural).

Mark therefore indicates at least two strippings (and possibly three) associated with the flogging and mockery of Jesus in the *praetorium*. Matthew's account offers more detail and clarity. In Matthew's account, the first stripping (associated with the flogging) is implied, and the second and third strippings in the *praetorium* are explicit. Both Mark's account and Matthew's account agree that Jesus was reclothed in his own clothes for his journey through the city out to Golgotha. Mark 15:20 and Matthew 27:31 both end their accounts of the *praetorium* with Jesus being led away to be crucified. This signals a further stripping which is to take place at the place of the cross. This means that in Matthew 27:26–31 there are references to four different strippings of Jesus, and in Mark 15:15–20 there are references to at least three different strippings. In each version, all these references are stated with economy and conveyed in just six verses.

An especially disturbing detail in the accounts in Mark and Matthew is that both explicitly state that it was the *whole cohort* (*speira*) of Roman soldiers—that is, about 500 men—that was assembled.[11] This was an overwhelming show of force against a single prisoner. As a hostile display of military power, it sounds a particularly disturbing note. Commentators sometimes understate the acutely threatening events in the *praetorium* by using euphemistic language suggestive of spontaneous 'horseplay' or 'buffoonery', or by likening the mockery to comedy, carried out by a small group. The indication that 500 soldiers were present suggests that something much more organised and more sinister was taking place. The language of 'called together' (Mark 15:16) or 'gathered' (Matt. 27:27) suggests something more orchestrated and significant.

The Stripping at the Cross

Most scholars believe that victims of Roman crucifixions were naked. Ancient writers outside the gospels provide support for this belief, and it is further evidenced in the understanding of early Christian authors.

Dionysius of Halicarnassus, a rhetorician living in Rome and writing in Greek in the first century BCE, describes a slave being driven through Rome to his execution by other slaves (*Roman Antiquities*, 7.69.1–2). He writes:

> The men ordered to lead the slave to his punishment, having stretched out both his arms and fastened them to a piece of wood which extended across his breast and shoulders as far as his wrists, followed him, tearing his naked body with whips.

Dionysius says the slave was marched in this manner through the Forum and 'every other conspicuous part of the city'. It is not explicit in this passage that the slave was fully naked or that the manner of execution is crucifixion. However, the fact that the victim is a slave, and is carrying a beam or wooden fork or yoke (*furca*) suggests crucifixion (because crucifixion was 'slaves' punishment'). In an aside, Dionysius notes that 'the culprit, overcome by such cruelty, not only uttered ill-omened cries, forced from him by the pain, but also made indecent movements under the blows'. The mention of these 'indecent' movements in response to the blows makes most sense if the slave was naked and suggests the sexually charged ethos of the scene.[12]

Artemidorus Daldianus, a mid-second-century diviner in Ephesus who wrote a five-volume work in Greek titled *Oneirocritica* or 'The Interpretation of Dreams', reports that 'the crucified are stripped naked and lose their flesh' (*Oneirocritica* 2.53). The loss of flesh most probably refers to the carrion birds or other animals attracted by the bleeding flesh from the flogging. A body on the cross was defenceless even whilst still alive.

There are only a few depictions of crucifixion from the first five centuries to provide visual evidence either for or against nudity. Crucifixion was not typically shown in Roman art and initially avoided also in Christian art until the fifth century. It was not until well after Constantine's mother Helena had apparently 'discovered' a relic of the True Cross in Jerusalem (320 CE) and Constantine had abolished crucifixion as a punishment (337 CE) that the cross starts to be included in Christian art from the fifth century onwards. One of the most consistent conventions—extending from these earliest Christian images to the present—is that Jesus on the cross is depicted as wearing a loincloth (*subligaculum*) rather than being shown as fully naked. This artistic convention has had a powerful impact on the conventional understanding of crucifixion in modernity, even though there is no mention of any loincloth in the canonical gospels. The apocryphal Gospel of Nicodemus (1:10) refers to the soldiers putting a linen cloth (*lention*) on Jesus after stripping him at the cross (Ehrman and Pleše 2011, 443). However, this gospel—also known as the Acts of Pilate—was written centuries after the event.[13]

The loincloth in Christian art is motivated more by respect than historical accuracy (Wijngaards 1995). Two early non-Christian images—the Pereire gem and the Palatine graffito, which are discussed in Chapter 3—depict Jesus as exposed.[14] The Pereire gem from the late second or early third century features a figure presumed to be Jesus naked on a cross. The Palatine graffito, from approximately the same time, shows a crucified figure viewed from behind. He has the head of an ass and seems to be wearing a tunic down to his hips but is naked from the hips down. This image is sometimes cited as counter evidence for the view that crucifixion involved nudity. However, even if the figure is wearing a tunic there is no sign of a loincloth. On the contrary, the image shows the buttocks exposed, and therefore presumably the genitals exposed as well.

The evidence that Jesus was fully naked is also supported in the New Testament and from early Christian writings. Paul speaks of Jesus as the last Adam (1 Cor. 15:45) and sees this as especially important for understanding the significance of Jesus' death. Paul writes, 'For since death came through a human being, the resurrection of the dead has also come through a human being; for as all die in Adam, so all will be made alive in Christ' (1 Cor. 15:21–22). Adam and Eve were fully naked in his pre-Fall state, and knew no shame at this point (Gen. 2:25), however, after the Fall they realised they were naked (Gen. 3:7). Paul's words on Jesus as the last Adam fit with an understanding of Jesus as naked on the cross, and this reflects the sense of shame Paul associates with sin, nakedness, and crucifixion.[15]

Augustine develops this in his discussion of the nakedness of Noah. He describes Noah's shameful nakedness when asleep drunk (Gen. 9:20–25) as prefiguring Christ's humiliation in the Passion. He writes: 'the passion of Christ, which was signified by that man's [Noah's] nakedness' (*City of God*, 16.2.2). Noah's nakedness after drinking prompts Augustine to reflect on Jesus drinking the cup of suffering and to link this to Paul's words that Christ was 'crucified in weakness' (2 Cor. 13:4):

> He [Christ] has assumed flesh and blood that He might suffer; 'and he was drunken', that is, He suffered; 'and was naked', that is, His weakness appeared in His suffering, as the apostle says, 'though He was crucified through weakness'.[16]

Augustine is not alone in believing Jesus was naked on the cross. Other Early Christian writers took the nakedness of Jesus on the cross for granted. Melito of Sardis, writing in Greek in the second century, gave Christ's nakedness as the reason for the darkness at noon (Matt. 27:45). Melito writes in section 97 of *On Pascha*:

> O unprecedented murder! Unprecedented crime!
> The Sovereign has been made unrecognisable by his naked body,
> and is not even allowed a garment to keep him from view.
> That is why the luminaries turned away,
> and the day was darkened,
> so that he might hide the one stripped bare upon the tree,
> darkening not the body of the Lord
> but the eyes of men.
>
> (Melito of Sardis 1979, 55)

There is further support for Jesus' nakedness in the gospel texts, which record that after putting Jesus on the cross, the soldiers took his clothes to divide among themselves (Matt. 27:35; Mark 15:24; Luke 23:34; John 19:23). There is no mention of a loincloth remaining or a linen cloth being offered. The implication of nakedness is most explicit is John 19:23–24, which says that after dividing Jesus' clothes the soldiers then threw lots for his tunic (*chiton*) so as not to tear it. Although the possibility that Jesus might still have retained some clothing cannot be excluded beyond doubt, it would go against the reading of John 19:24 and the understanding of early Christian writers. It would also have been a very strange concession from the Romans, if the purpose of crucifixion was to inflict maximum humiliation. Whilst there might be good reason to include a loincloth in visual depictions of Jesus, to preserve his modesty and dignity—a point to which I will return in Chapter 4—this should not fool the viewer of these depictions into thinking that Jesus was actually afforded such respect. The dignity that the loincloth seeks to preserve is precisely the dignity that the Romans sought to strip away.

Taken together the Roman sources, the gospel texts, and the early Christian writings all point in the same direction as the Palatine graffito and Pereire gem. This provides a firm basis to conclude that Jesus was crucified naked and that this was most likely in line with common Roman practice. Nudity was an intentional, even strategic, part of punishment and carried a strong and readily recognisable public message. Finney writes: 'Hence, those prisoners who were stripped naked before scourging and crucified naked in public places, suffered as much from the shame of involuntary nakedness as from the lash' (Finney 2013, 127).

Some commentators suggest that the Romans might have treated the Jews differently at crucifixion, because of Jewish sensitivity regarding nakedness. The beheading of the tribune Celer is sometimes given in support of this. Josephus describes Celer as being dragged through the city and beheaded (c. 50 CE), but he makes no mention of Celer being disrobed or naked (*War*, 2.12.7; *Ant*. 20.6.3). Yet even if the inference that Celer remained clothed is correct, and the passage's silence is hardly conclusive, a more plausible explanation is that Celer's status as a tribune might have warranted a greater measure of decorum than was shown to the condemned in crucifixions. Beheading was a more dignified and honourable execution than crucifixion, and the treatment of Celer should not be seen as direct evidence for how Jewish victims of crucifixion were treated. There is no reason to think that such respect would have been offered to Jesus or to the two criminals crucified alongside him.

To sum up, the gospels indicate that Jesus was clothed during his journey to execution but was then stripped a final time at the cross and crucified naked. Furthermore, whilst it is true that Jewish sensitivities around naked exposure were high, this could have been all the more reason to enforce the stripping at the cross rather than to waive it. If the purpose of stripping was humiliation, then it is unlikely that the Romans would have desisted because it was seen as especially humiliating (Tombs 2020a, 47–48). The Romans do not seem to have afforded the early Christians any concession along these lines. In the early fourth century, Phileas Bishop of Thmuis (Egypt) complained that the chief outrage to the

Christian martyrs was that after torture their disfigured and naked corpses were displayed in public (Eusebius, *Hist. Eccl.* 8.10; cited Coleman 1990, 49). Further evidence for this comes from Ambrose of Milan (340–397 CE), who claims that male lions did not gaze at a naked female virgin martyr during the martyrdoms of earlier times. Whether or not Ambrose's understanding of the modesty of lions is plausible, his words are revealing in regard to his belief in the nudity of martyrs (*De virginibus*, 2.3.20).

In the absence of other evidence there is no reason to think that Jesus or other Jews were given a special dispensation to remain clothed during crucifixion. As will be discussed in Chapter 3, in the ancient world crucifixion was viewed with a strong sense of horror. The naked vulnerability of the victim was an integral part of the shame crucifixion involves. If the purpose was to humiliate the victim, full nakedness would have been effective in both the Jewish and Roman cultural contexts. The strong sense of humiliation would have made the use of enforced nudity *more* likely, rather than less likely.

Stripping, Enforced Nudity, and Sexual Abuse

Gourevitch and Morris report that when they interviewed Lynndie England about sexual abuses at Abu Ghraib, she dismissed the idea that stripping the prisoner they called 'Gus' was sexual humiliation. She asked why someone would think this, and asked in reply 'Just because Gus is naked?' In her eyes, it had not been *sexual* humiliation because 'that's standard operating procedure' (Gourevitch and Morris 2008, 139).

Presenting the stripping of Jesus as a form of sexualised violence, and therefore as sexual abuse, is often met with similar scepticism. I have often been told that this confuses the past with the present. It is, in my experience, quite common for someone to suggest that although the gospel depictions might be judged as suggestive of sexual abuse if assessed by today's standards, they would not have been viewed as sexual abuse in the first century.

One area of confusion that might contribute to this response is a conflation of voluntary unclothing and forced stripping. I do not say that the simple fact of being unclothed equates to or suggests humiliation or sexual abuse. In everyday life, there are situations in which undressing voluntarily is routine and there is no reason to think of it as either disturbing or abusive. However, the level of coercion and control at Abu Ghraib was very different from situations where people undress by choice or for practical reasons. The nudity at Abu Gharib was *not* voluntary but enforced. The elements of choice and control are crucial contextual factors in thinking about how stripping and nudity are to be understood—both at Abu Ghraib and in the gospel accounts.

Another reason that has been given for arguing that Jesus was not a victim of sexual abuse is that his mistreatment was not for sexual gratification. This seems to rest on an unduly restrictive definition of sexual abuse. Whilst sexual gratification certainly provides a motivation for sexual abuse, it is a mistake to insist that it is an essential criterion. To do so gives too much emphasis to a perpetrator's motivations and not enough to a victim's experience. If it happens today, how is a victim likely to experience the crimes perpetrated against Jesus? Would they feel the public display by a hostile force to be humiliating and harmful to their sense of personal dignity and sexual integrity? If so, it is appropriate to name the violation as a form of sexual abuse. The same is true for the first century.

As noted earlier in this chapter, when a prisoner first enters a detention facility, they may be stripped for legitimate security reasons. Even so, it is important to consider the impact that this has on them. Even if the stripping is *intended* as part of a legitimate security procedure, it can still have a traumatic impact if it violates a prisoner's wishes and leaves them feeling humiliated and vulnerable. Stripping takes away protection, takes away dignity, and takes away humanity. In such cases, even a legally sanctioned stripping of a prisoner is no small matter. It may sometimes be necessary, but the perceived security benefits should be weighed against the impact this has on the prisoner and their sense of self. Furthermore, just because some uses of stripping in detention may be for a legitimate and appropriate purpose, this does not mean that there is a legitimate motive behind every stripping. The systematic use of nudity at Abu Ghraib suggests that the stripping of prisoners was *not* intended for security but for humiliation. The photo of the naked Abu Ghraib prisoner on a leash does not come close to a legitimate instance of stripping. For a naked prisoner in this setting, the language of sexual abuse is appropriate. There is no genital touching in the scene, nor any suggestion of obvious sexual gratification, but there can be no question that it is a form of sexualised mistreatment that amounts to abuse. To name the nature of this abuse more specifically as 'sexual abuse' is not speculative or irresponsible. It is an appropriate recognition of what is happening, why it is happening, and, very probably, of how it is experienced by the victim. The naked exposure of the prisoner has meaning and purpose. It is tied to their identity and dignity, and it deliberately and strategically displays their vulnerability in a sexually charged way.

Sandesh Sivakumaran identifies the targeting of sexuality as the key to understanding what constitutes sexual violence. He describes sexual violence as 'any violence, physical or psychological, carried out through sexual means or by targeting sexuality' (Sivakumaran 2007, 261). Stripping and enforced nudity have a psychological impact precisely because they are targeted at the victim's sexual identity and increase sexual vulnerability.

A policy report from the International Criminal Court explains that 'sexual crimes' under its jurisdiction—which include rape, sex trafficking, enforced prostitution, and sexual violence—are concerned with acts of a 'sexual nature' against a person. Sexual crimes, therefore, cover both physical and non-physical acts with a sexual element. It explains: 'An act of a sexual nature is not limited to physical violence, and may not involve any physical contact—for example, forced nudity' (Office of the Prosecutor 2014). The key factor in this understanding is not whether the act was carried out for the sexual gratification of the perpetrator but whether or not it involved a sexual element. Forced nudity is explicitly recognised as a possible example of this.

Whether or not forced nudity constitutes a crime or not will depend on the specific context. Ní Aoláin explains that attention to forced nudity is relatively recent under international law and awareness has grown since the 1990s, as seen in cases at both the International Criminal Tribunal for Rwanda (ICTR) and the International Criminal Tribunal for the former Yugoslavia (ICTY). As a result, Ní Aoláin says, there is now 'a far more nuanced understanding of the scope and content of sexual violence and its multiple permutations' (Ní Aoláin 2016). She cites the ICTR precedent, where the tribunal judged that the forced undressing of a victim can be a crime against humanity. It also recognised that coercion could take different forms. For military personnel to be present during a stripping, their presence could be judged as coercive even if they do not use direct physical force. Ní Aoláin also notes that at the ICTY, the Kunarac Court set two criteria for judging whether outrages upon personal dignity reached a criminal threshold. The barrier for humiliation was set high: 'the humiliation of the victim must be so intense that any reasonable person would be outraged' (Ní Aoláin 2016).

The use of stripping and enforced nudity as sexual violence is recognised in The Hague Principles on Sexual Violence. These Principles were drawn up through a collaboration in 2019 between lawyers, representatives of 60 civil society organisations, and over 500 survivors of sexual violence.[17] The Principles interpret sexual violence broadly as encompassing 'all violations of sexual autonomy and sexual integrity' (Women's Initiatives for Gender Justice 2019, 5). They note that sexual violence is often characterised by humiliation, domination, and destruction, and it does not need to have a sexual motivation (Women's Initiatives for Gender Justice 2019, 11). In their list of indicators that characterise acts of a sexual nature, the first indicator lists exposing a sexual body part (Women's Initiatives for Gender Justice 2019, 26).

Recognising gendered power dynamics in the stripping of a Roman political prisoner is not an anachronistic projection from recent events to a distant past. The significance of stripping would have been readily understandable to a Roman audience. In fact, a Roman audience would most likely see stripping as more deeply humiliating than a western audience would see it today. Jonathan Walters explains that the Roman sexual protocol that defined men as 'impenetrable penetrators' should be seen in the context of a wider conceptual pattern that characterises true men as 'being able to defend the boundaries of their body from invasive assaults of all kinds' (Walters 1997, 30). The importance placed on penetration within Roman attitudes to sex carried over to other forms of bodily penetration and gave them a more sexualised significance in Roman eyes than would be usual in modern western societies. The forms of penetration involved in stripping, beating, and piercing would therefore, in all likelihood, have had a much stronger sexualised element in their Roman context in comparison with what is seen today as sexual contact.

It is therefore understandable that in recent years a growing number of scholars and commentators are giving increased attention to the act of stripping in the mistreatment of Jesus. They recognise that attention to the sexual significance and gender values in stripping is not a distortion of how those involved in the stripping of Jesus would have seen it but a necessary part of understanding how it appeared to those who were involved, including its traumatic impact on those involved as witnesses (O'Donnell 2021). Michael Trainor concludes: 'In a powerful and public way, it was an act of sexual abuse' (Trainor 2014, 42). Likewise, Chris Greenough makes clear that 'enforced nudity, is without doubt, sexual abuse. It has the strategy of shaming, humiliating, and disempowering its victim' (Greenough 2021, 62). Hilary Scarsella writes: 'We can say confidently, then, that Jesus's crucifixion was sexually violent. Jesus was a victim of sexual violence' (Scarsella 2020, 156). Carolyn Mackie writes, 'The Gospel writers tell us that Jesus was stripped naked publicly, a form of sexual abuse by any standards' (Mackie 2021).

Conclusion

Sabrina Harman wrote to her partner about an experience from Abu Ghraib that left a strong impression on her:

> I walk down stairs after blowing the whistle and beating on the cells with an asp [baton] to find 'the taxicab driver' handcuffed backwards to his window naked with his underwear over his head and face. He looked like Jesus Christ.
> (Gourevitch and Morris 2006, 110)

It is easy to read the Bible without realising that the sexual abuse shown in photos of Abu Ghraib is also present in the New Testament. Stripping a prisoner naked is a deliberate form of abuse. What we see in the photos of naked men at Abu Ghraib is rightly denounced as sexual humiliation. Strangely, however, the very similar treatment of Jesus of Nazareth seems often to go unnoticed and unremarked upon. Why is this? It was surely as shameful in first-century Palestine for the Romans to strip and display a Jewish man naked as it is for US forces to do this to Muslim prisoners in twenty-first-century Iraq. If the Bible is read carefully, and taken seriously, the stripping of Jesus can be seen for what it really is: sexualised violence as a form of punitive humiliation. It is appropriate to identify this as a form of sexual abuse.

I argue that it is important to acknowledge the sexual humiliation revealed in the text. Furthermore, acknowledgement of the stripping and enforced nudity as sexual abuse is long overdue and provides a firm basis for recognising Jesus as a victim of sexual abuse and addressing the implications of this for the church as 'the body of Christ' (1 Cor. 12:27). However, in addition to what the texts reveal, violence that the texts might conceal also needs attention. There may have been a level of sexual abuse in the *praetorium* that none of the gospels explicitly discloses. This possibility is addressed in the next chapter.

Notes

1 Amongst the extensive media coverage on the Abu Ghraib photos and the prisoner abuse they depict, see especially the work of Danner (2004). On the shifts in US policy that led to Abu Ghraib, see especially Hersh (2004).
2 Adb is the naked figure wearing only a dark hood with his hand on his genitals in a widely publicised photo featuring the guard Pfc. Lynndie England: https://commons.wikimedia.org/wiki/File:AG-10.jpg.
3 The discussion of attitudes presented in this section is largely restricted to evidence offered by the Hebrew Bible, but other Jewish sources would offer further support for this argument as well; see especially Boyarin (1993). The first-century Jewish historian Josephus attests to the stigma of genital exposure when he speaks of the dishonour a person suffers if their genitals 'offend the rays of the deity' (Josephus, *War* 2.148).
4 Leviticus 20:17 equates the idiom of seeing nakedness with uncovering nakedness, whilst in Leviticus 18:6 and Ezekiel 16:36–37, 22:10, 23:10, 23:18, and 23:29, the term 'uncovering nakedness' is also used for sexual intercourse. The possibility of maternal incest is based on Leviticus 18:7–8, where the 'the nakedness of your mother' is described as the 'nakedness of your father' (likewise in Lev. 18:14 and 18:16, and also Lev. 20:11 and 20:21).
5 Barbara Thiede writes: 'The king of the ancient Near East is a warrior among warriors, a man who feminizes as well as kills his enemies. Enemies are ridiculed, cursed, shamed, and mutilated. They are dubbed passive and weak, and described as women'; Thiede (2022, 72). See also Chapman (2004) and Winkler (2020).
6 The Seleucid ruler Antiochus IV Epiphanes (175–164 BCE) gave the Jewish High Priest Jason permission to build a gymnasium in Jerusalem (Josephus, *Antiquities* 12.236). However, the Hellenised Jews who reversed their circumcision so as to exercise at the gymnasium unclothed were condemned as apostates by both Josephus and the authors of 1 and 2 Maccabees (1 Macc. 1:10–15; 2 Macc. 4.7–17).
7 The symposium originally served an educational purpose in inducting younger men into adult society. The word 'symposium' derives from 'drinking together', and the gatherings were elaborate social events. Greek pottery shows men at symposia reclining naked on couches. The guests are all male and are attended by male and female slaves, who are also shown naked. Some vases depict sexual relations between guests and those who served them. Although some caution is required before concluding that the images on vases necessarily correspond with the reality of a symposium, it is likely that the symposia were another social context where nudity was permissible and even celebrated.
8 Pertinent here is the Roman concern for *dignitas* and *impudicita*. Roman *dignitas* has no direct English equivalent, but it covers an individual's dignity, public standing and respect, social merit, honour, and the expectation of self-control (Williams 2010, 219–223).
9 See also Edwards and Tombs (2018). Reaves and Tombs (2019) reviews the presentation of Jesus as a victim of sexual abuse in the works by Tombs (1999), Trainor (2014), Heath (2011), and Gafney (2013).
10 Flogging was intended to pierce the skin, and so it would make little sense to flog a victim who has clothing to offer some (albeit limited) protection. In addition, if the flogging is severe, then any clothing that the victim is still wearing would be pulled to shreds, which would ensure they were stripped by the end even if not at the start. A plausible explanation for the parallel strips which appear on the Puteoli graffito (discussed in Chapter 3) is that these depict the flogging of the victim prior to crucifixion.

If so, they suggest that the whole body was flogged, and the victim was not wearing clothing.

11 A cohort was one-tenth of a legion and in the first century consisted of about 500 men (Luz 1989, 513 fn 9). Many commentators suggest that a smaller unit than a cohort must be intended, or perhaps only part of a cohort. The wording 'the whole cohort' (*holēn ten speiran*) is against the reading of the verse as intending only part of a cohort. In most other cases in the New Testament, *speira* is used in contexts where 500 soldiers seem appropriate. One likely exception to this usage is John 18:3, where *speira* is used for the soldiers who arrest Jesus. In this case, a lesser number seems likely to ensure a low-profile night-time arrest. In the *praetorium* the whole cohort could be assembled without this concern, and given the language in both Mark and Matthew, it is reasonable to believe that this was a whole cohort of about 500 men. The assumption that a smaller number is intended may reflect the mistaken belief that the events in the *praetorium* are unimportant.

12 A later passage in Dionysius refers to an uprising in Rhegium (*Roman Antiquities*, 20.16.1). After it was quashed, a large group of prisoners were taken in chains to Rome. The senate decreed execution, and 300 prisoners at a time were tied naked to stakes in the Forum with their elbows behind them. After they had been scourged 'in front of all', the tendons of their necks were cut with an axe and the prisoners replaced with another 300 (*Roman Antiquities*, 20.16.2). This second passage is not a conventional crucifixion scene, but it is further evidence that Dionysius viewed enforced and displayed nudity as part of the punishment for both slaves and prisoners in the lead-up to their execution.

13 The Gospel of Nicodemus is written in Greek but claims to have originally been composed in Hebrew. It is hard to date, but the fourth century is likely, and possibly later; see Ehrman and Pleše (2011, 420).

14 For the Pereire gem, see www.britishmuseum.org/collection/object/H_1986-0501-1, and for the Palatine graffito, see https://commons.wikimedia.org/wiki/File:Alexorig.jpg.

15 See Jeremy Punt, 'Knowing Christ Crucified (1 Corinthians 2:2): Cross, Humiliation and Humility', in Reaves et al. (2021: 91–109).

16 Augustine goes on to offer the mistaken claim that Scripture makes a parallel between how Noah was naked 'in his house' and how Jesus was mistreated by the Jews. This quite wrongly blames the Jews rather than the Romans for Jesus' nakedness.

17 Women's Initiatives for Gender Justice, *The Hague Principles on Sexual Violence* (Hague: Women's Initiatives for Gender Justice, 2019): https://thehagueprinciples.org.

2 The Mocking

'.. and mocked him ...'

(Matt. 27:29)

Introduction

In Christian tradition, the 'way of the cross' has been represented many thousands of times in imaginative renderings in art, liturgies, and prayer, to mark and remember the path leading to the execution of Jesus in Jerusalem. The way of the cross invites Christians to a painful scrutiny of the journey that Jesus took to his death, and to accompany him as a community of faith. Following in his steps can also focus attention on some deeply disturbing practices in both the ancient and modern world. This chapter and the next examine whether Jesus might have been subjected to further sexual assault beyond the stripping in the *praetorium*. These further questions cannot be avoided, and the issues they raise are disturbing.

This might be the point where you stop—or least pause—in your reading. You may prefer to read Chapter 4 instead: on why and how the acknowledgement of Jesus as a victim of sexualised violence—whatever form this experience took—can be seen as potentially meaningful. You may decide that it is both unnecessary and unhelpful to investigate whether Jesus experienced further sexual assault—either in the *praetorium* or at the cross. You may feel that working towards a constructive response to sexual violence is a better next step than delving deeper into the possibility of further suffering.

If you decide to continue, the evidence of further sexual assault in the mocking and crucifixion is less clear-cut than the evidence for stripping discussed in Chapter 1. There is sufficient evidence to raise confronting questions on both the mocking and the crucifixion, but not enough to find definitive answers. For those who want certainties these chapters may be frustrating. However, there are good reasons for at least raising the questions and then carefully assessing available evidence even if the investigation is unlikely to prove conclusive. This is not a unique problem to an investigation of crucifixion. Biblical scholars face this challenge in much of their work across a range of topics. The priority when only partial evidence—or contradictory evidence—is available should be to be as honest

DOI: 10.4324/9780429289750-3

to it as possible and to acknowledge when gaps and uncertainties remain. The intention of undertaking this chapter is to take seriously the evidence which is available. This can be a form of discipleship in following Jesus on the way of the cross. A caution, though, that it is a journey that should only be taken alongside a commitment to self-care.

Following the same approach as Chapter 1, this chapter starts with the mistreatment of prisoners as documented in recent reports. While accounts of prisoner abuse in recent decades cannot answer all questions about prisoner mistreatment in the first century, they can stimulate an empathetic imagination and give us ways to engage more deeply with biblical texts and other ancient sources. Recent reports show that in many cases after a prisoner is stripped, he or she is subjected to further forms of sexual violence and degradation. This opens up possibilities that Jesus might also have been subjected to further sexual violence after the stripping, and it is appropriate to ask what this might have involved.

The chapter then gives context from the ancient world on sexual violence against captives and enslaved people. Last, attention is given to two accounts of mockery and sexual violence that might offer context for reading the mocking of Jesus. The first is the story of the Levite's wife in Judges 19; the second is the mockery and insults perpetrated by soldiers after the death of Herod Agrippa.

Taking the contextual and textual evidence together, it is, I argue, neither unduly speculative nor irresponsible to conclude that further sexual assault *may* have taken place in the *praetorium*. My hope is that an inter-reading of modern and ancient accounts will encourage more sensitivity to the possibilities of recognising sexual violence also in the gospel accounts.

Sexualised Violence Against Male Detainees

Sexual violence against prisoners has been common throughout history; however, it is only relatively recently that it has received sustained attention. Susan Brownmiller's groundbreaking work on rape published in 1975 offers an overview of sexual violence during armed conflicts, including World War I, World War II, Bangladesh (1971), and Vietnam (1965–73; Brownmiller 1975, 31–113). From the early 1990s attention to sexual violence against women as an intentional weapon of war started to gain momentum. This was largely because of the sexual violence against female prisoners that was widely reported in Bosnia (1992–95) and Rwanda (1994). Since the mid-1990s, great strides have been made around public awareness on sexual violence in wartime settings against women (Lamb 2020).

Since 2012, the subject of sexual violence against male victims has also started to receive more public attention (Schulz 2016; Dolan 2018; Zalewski et al. 2018; Schulz 2021). Most commentators note that information on the prevalence of conflict-related sexual violence against male detainees is even harder to gather than figures on the rape of women in detention. As Du Toit and Le Roux (2020) discuss, one difficulty is the stigma associated with sexual violence generally, which has additional aspects for male victims because of heteronormative expectations around masculine identity.

One conclusion emerges clearly from available studies: the issue of power and control is just as important for an understanding of sexual violence against men as it is for understanding sexual violence against women. Put another way, sexual gratification is not a necessary requirement for the abuse inflicted in detention to constitute sexualised violence.[1] It is possible that some guards might derive sexual gratification from sexualised violence—or at least some form of psychological gratification from their role in inflicting sexual harm. However, there are other priorities in inflicting sexualised violence in detention regardless of any sexual gratification. It is primarily a display of power and control and a form of humiliation. It is directed against a particularly vulnerable element in the prisoner: their sexual and their gender identity.

Reports indicate that the overwhelming majority of sexualised abuses in detention are committed by male guards rather than female guards, although there are documented cases of female guards initiating or assisting in such abuse, as they did at Abu Ghraib (Sjoberg 2014, 73). Sexual violence against a male detainee is a way for those in power to claim, demonstrate, and enforce power and control in line with the values of hegemonic masculinity (Ganzevoort and Sremac 2016). These meanings can be amplified through collective action, including gang rape, where guards develop and consolidate bonds with each other through, for instance, the rape of a vulnerable prisoner.[2] The normalisation within patriarchy of diminishing a women through violence can feed the perception that an abused male prisoner is 'like a woman'. This in turn, allows those involved to understand themselves as acting in a 'manly' way in line with heteronormative expectations (Tombs 2002b).

In some cases, perceived stigma or discrimination may restrain male guards from raping male captives. In such cases, however, the guards may choose instead to force other prisoners to take on the role of rapist. Another common practice is to use objects or weapons as instruments of penetration. For example, in October 2011, Channel 4 television news (in the UK) broadcast brief video footage from the online news site GlobalPost, which recorded an attack on Muammar Gaddafi following his capture near Sirte a few days before (Channel 4 News 2011). The video showed Gaddafi being anally assaulted with a weapon or instrument, most likely a bayonet (HRW 2012).

Recent torture reports attest that stripping and nudity are *first steps* towards other forms of sexual abuse. A study of Sri Lankan detainees conducted by the Medical Foundation for the Care of Victims of Torture (London) explains:

> Sexual abuse in detention starts with forced nudity, which many of the Sri Lankan detainees described. This is usually associated with verbal sexual threats and mocking, which adds to the humiliation and degradation of being tortured.
>
> (Peel et al. 2000, 2069)

In Sri Lankan detention, genital beating, genital mutilation, and castration are all documented alongside rape and sexual penetration with instruments.

30 *The Mocking*

At Bagram air base in Afghanistan in 2002, too, when US military police (MPs) stripped Afghan captives, the action of stripping immediately raised the fear of other forms of sexual assault:

> Rubber-gloved MPs armed with surgical scissors made them [the prisoners] lie on their stomachs and began cutting away the rags. At the first snip of the scissors, the prisoners howled and wailed and struggled to roll over, fearing there could only be one purpose for being held facedown and stripped. The screaming stirred the line of prisoners still waiting in the reception area to states of supreme agitation.
>
> (Mackey and Miller 2004, 4)

This may have been an intentional use of an implied threat of further violence. It also had the additional impact of provoking fear and anxiety in other prisoners within earshot.

Modern accounts of torture attest to many different forms of sexualised violence. When electrocution is used against prisoners, it is common for it to be used against sensitive body parts including the genitals. For example, many testimonies to torture during the military dictatorship in Brazil make reference to electrical shocks to the genitals. This included prisoners being strapped to a special chair—the so-called Dragon's Chair—and electrical shocks to the whole body were supplemented by targeted shocks to the genitals. Other tortures included genital beatings, and the sexualised use of animals and insects, including cockroaches and snakes (Archdiocese of Sao Paulo 1986, 16–24).

A similar pattern of sexualised brutality is shown in reports from Argentina (CONADEP 1986, 34 File No. 5552). A commonly used instrument for administering electric shocks in Argentina was *la picana*, a small, electrified prod. The phallic shape of the prod was highly suggestive of the sexual element in this torture (Graziano 1992, 153–158). The use of *la picana* in the rape and sexual abuse of women has been well documented. Two Argentinean male victims also witness to how shocks with *la picana* eventually escalated to anal rape (CONADEP 1986, 24). In El Salvador in the 1980s, the aftermath of extreme genital violence against both women and men was often displayed in public. Sexually mutilated bodies were often left in public places as warnings to others (Tombs 2006).

Other forms of sexual violence also followed the stripping at Abu Ghraib. Gourevitch and Morris write (2008, 185): 'Brutality is boring ... you stripped them of their pride. There wasn't much more you could take away from them, but people are inventive'. For example, on the night of 7 November 2003 naked detainees were assembled into a human pyramid and photographed. Later that night, in the early hours of the morning of 8 November, they were forced into positions to masturbate or perform oral sex on other prisoners (Gourevitch and Morris 2008, 187). In another example of escalation, the previous chapter notes that Sabrina Harman describes in a letter home how the vulnerability of a naked prisoner known as the 'taxicab driver' reminded her of Jesus. What happened next indicates the easy escalation of sexual humiliation when victims are naked:

> He looked like Jesus Christ. At first I had to laugh so I went on and grabbed the camera and took a picture. One of the guys took my asp [baton] and started 'poking' at his dick.
>
> (Gourevitch and Morris 2008, 110)

Here, the vulnerability of the naked prisoner raised the likelihood and ease of sexualised assault. In other photos from the prison, intimidation and threat of danger to the prisoners are especially clear as naked prisoners cower in front of dogs.

After the initial outcry over the photos of naked prisoners at Abu Ghraib had subsided, subsequent reports emerged of additional sexual violence and humiliations there, including acts of sexual penetration using objects and instruments. Photos of this are reported to exist but have not been released. The reason given for this is the damage it would cause to the reputation of the United States in the Middle East, and the fear of future retribution against US personnel (Relman 2016).

To sum up, sexual violence beyond stripping is widespread during torture and detention in the present day and can be evidenced in widely different contexts and cultures. However, it often receives little more than generic acknowledgement unless a conscious effort is made to investigate and expose specific practices. Given the prevalence of such violence today, largely unacknowledged or covered only in the less specific language of 'torture', it is reasonable to ask whether an investigation of first-century Roman practices might expose something similar about how captives were mistreated.

Sexualised Violence Against Roman Captives

Sexual violence against war captives was neither remarkable nor exceptional in Roman eyes.[3] Cicero's account of the capture of Syracuse by Marcellus (212 BCE) refers to the rape of freeborn families and married women as 'a custom of war and the right of a conqueror' (*Against Verres*, 2.4.116).

The close connection between rape and capture is indicated in the Latin verb *rapere*. Originally *rapere* meant 'to seize and carry off' a woman. Rome's foundation legend is the rape of the Sabine women in c. 750 BCE (Hemker 1985). Over time the term *rapere* was extended to include forced sexual intercourse without abduction (as in the rape of Lucretia, c. 509 BCE). Rape laws offered some protection to women in respectable families but these did not extend to enslaved people, sex workers, and other professions considered to be disreputable (Burgess-Jackson 1999, 16; Nguyen 2006). In 54 BCE, Cicero successfully defended the politician, Gnaeus Plancius, against the accusation that when Plancius was a youth he raped a young mime actress. Actresses were seen as disreputable, and Cicero dismissed the rape as 'an act which he was permitted by privilege to commit' (*Pro Plancio* 30).[4]

In the sacking of a city, the 'privilege' of rape was extended much more widely, and the inhabitants had little protection from victorious soldiers. Then as now, many of these rapes would have been opportunistic and motivated by sexual gratification. However, sexual violence must always be scrutinised in relation to power dynamics. Indeed, expression of power and dominance supersedes expression of sexual gratification or sexual orientation according to the bulk of modern sexuality research on rape. In modern conflicts (REMHI 1999, 77–78; Zarkov 2001) and in Roman times (Walters 1997), rape and other forms of sexual violence demonstrate the conquest and denigration of an enemy as a vanquished 'other'. Sexual assaults in that context express the Roman attitudes to penetrative hegemonic masculinity discussed in Chapter 1. In addition, in many cases, sexualised violence is reinforced by racialised notions of power, superiority, and otherness. This added a further power dynamic to the symbolism of rape and sexualised violence in warfare.[5]

Detailed descriptions of sexual violence in the sacking of a city are rare. However, this should not be taken as an indication that rape of captives was uncommon. Caryn Reeder notes that wartime rape of women is featured in different genres of Greek and Roman writings. The sources do not present rape as strange or feel the need to explain it. Livy's description of events after Hannibal took the town of Victumulae (219 BCE) during the Second Punic War (218–201 BCE) suggest that rape and other sexual violence was commonplace. Livy writes:

> A signal was suddenly given to the conquerors to pillage the place like a captured city. Nor were the people spared any of the atrocities usually recounted by historians as occurring in such circumstances. Indeed, the wretched inhabitants were subjected to every form of sexual abuse, cruelty, and inhuman mistreatment. Such were Hannibal's winter operations.
> (Livy, *History of Rome*, 21.57.14)

Livy also reports 'unspeakable abuse' against the Lorcians. The Lorcians had surrendered to the Carthaginians in 215 BCE but the town had been retaken by the Romans. The passage is unusual because it implies that the abuse was not only directed against the wives and children but against the men as well:

> Of all those things that make the strength of the powerful hateful to the weak there was not one overlooked by the commander or his men with regard to the townspeople: unspeakable abuse was inflicted on their persons, their children, and their wives.
> (Livy, *History of Rome*, 29.8.8)

Reeder notes that rape and sexual violence in war seem to have been taken for granted by Roman authors. What was seen as worth recording on the subject were the infrequent occasions when commanders and soldiers showed restraint (Reeder 2017, 364).

Julia Belser (2014) discusses how conquered nations are often represented in Roman art as the bodies of subjected women. Imperial triumph is signalled in explicitly sexual terms by placing the violated body of a conquered nation—depicted as female—at the mercy of the virile Roman conqueror. For example, the Roman conquest of Britannia by Claudius (43 CE) is depicted in a first-century marble relief in the street known as the Sebasteion (a Greek term for the Latin Augustus) in the town for Aphrodisias in Asia Minor (Tabeling 2020). This relief bears the inscription 'Claudius Caesar—Britannia'. Male Claudius is shown standing over female Britannia and is about to strike her with his right hand. His cloak covers his back but apart from the cloak and his helmet and weapons he is naked. His right knee presses down on Britannia's right hip as she lies beneath him; with his left hand he seems to be holding her head up by her hair. Britannia's right arm is raised as if to ward off the expected blow. She wears only a tunic, and it has either been torn or has slipped to expose her right breast. Britannia's vulnerability to naked aggression personifies the subjugated province. Today, most people would condemn a public monument that explicitly glorified sexualised violence. However, for the Roman Empire, the Sebasteion was intended to show both virtue and victory of Roman rulers. Representations of victory were meant to inscribe the virile glory of imperial might (Belser 2014, 9).

Rape of captives served an important political purpose (Gaca 2018). The inhabitants of a defeated city could expect to be taken into slavery. As enslaved people, they would have no choice but to serve the sexual wishes of their new masters (Glancy 2002, 27–29). Reeder (2017, 376–377) explains: 'The rape of the women and children of defeated enemies was a physical realization of their new status as slaves (The same would be true of men, though the rape of men is only rarely alluded to in the sources.).'. Sexual violence was used to demonstrate to the captives, and to a wider public, that they were now reduced in status from their previous standing.

A similar message of political and sexual submission is expressed in the rape of the daughters of Boudicca and Prasutagus. King Prasutagus of the Iceni had been a local ally to the Romans. When he died in c. 60 CE he named Nero as his heir along with his two daughters, in the hope that this arrangement would allow the alliance with Rome to continue and his daughters would take his place. Instead, the Romans enslaved members of his family, flogged Boudicca, publicly raped their two daughters, and confiscated Iceni lands 'as though they had been prizes of war' (Tacitus, *Annals* 14.31). Outraged by the mistreatment, and fearing worse to come, Boudicca rallied the Iceni and the neighbouring tribe Trinobantes into a bloody and ultimately unsuccessful revolt.

Tacitus' frank language '*violatae sunt*' on the violation of Boudicca's daughters leaves little doubt that they were raped. However, ancient sources are often more euphemistic. When rape or sexual violence is referenced in Roman elegies the account usually follows certain stylistic conventions to signal rape indirectly rather than explicitly. Writers speak of a woman's torn clothes, or dishevelled hair, so that a reader can infer rape (or attempted rape) without it being stated explicitly

(Fredrick 1997, 172). Similar conventions are observed by artists, as in the depiction of Britannica in the Sebasteion in Aphrodisias.

Sexual violence against male prisoners is barely mentioned in Roman writings.[6] Yet the dangers of male captive rape in war were sufficiently common for some allowances to be incorporated into the Roman legal code for freeborn male Romans who were raped as prisoners in wars, or when captured by pirates. These men were specifically exempted from the provision that men of *impudicitia* (immodesty)—that is, those who had been sexually penetrated—could not appear in court on behalf of others (Williams 2010, 214).

Slaves and prisoners were also subjected to other forms of sexual violence apart from rape, especially during judicial torture and punishment in the ancient world.[7] Torture in Rome was probably originally used for punishment (*tormentum*) but came to be used during judicial questioning (*quaestio*) of slaves and foreigners.

In her work on the 'fatal charades' of Roman punishments, Kathleen Coleman (1990, 44) discusses the second-century Christian writer Tertullian, who reported punishments he says he saw in the amphitheatre that were intended to re-enact popular mythic events. Tertullian writes, 'We have seen at one time or another Attis, that god from Pessinus, being castrated, and a man who was being burnt alive had taken on the role of Hercules' (Tertullian, *Apology*, 15.4–5).[8] Further research is required on the extent to which dismemberment and genital mutilation might have been used in Roman torture, but there is no reason to assume that Roman torture would have been more restrained than modern torture in this regard (REMHI 1999, 153).

To sum up, sexual violence against both female and male captives expressed important power dynamics. It demonstrated the power and virility of the penetrator and amplified the defeat, humiliation, and subjugation of the enemy. There is nothing in the Roman ethical or social code that would prevent—or even restrain—Roman soldiers from raping or abusing a captive condemned to crucifixion. Some of the Roman protocols around masculinity would actively support such abuses, especially when the victim was seen as defying the power and authority of Roman rule. In addition to this, torture against slaves and those condemned of crimes was widespread and often took extreme forms. In at least some cases, Roman torture of both female and male captives was highly sexualised.

The Mocking of Jesus

Testimonies from the present, writings from the past, and points of continuity between them are not sufficient in themselves to establish the historical facts of Jesus' suffering in the *praetorium*. However, they offer a reason for asking questions which might not otherwise be asked, and they can inform a sense of what is possible. This section turns to the biblical texts and the questions that might be asked. In particular, 'What else might the mockery in the *praetorium* have involved?' To answer this, this section looks especially at the accounts in Mark 15:16–20 and Matthew 27:26–31.

The *praetorium* was probably Herod's former palace on the western side of the city, or possibly the Antonia fortress on the corner of the Temple complex on the

The Mocking 35

eastern side of Jerusalem. In either case, it was enclosed, and the details of what happened inside are mostly hidden. They would probably not have been known with certainty even at the time. Furthermore, the gospels are usually seen as notably biased in excusing the Romans for Jesus' trial and death, and there would be good reason for reticence on such a shameful event.[9]

Neither Mark or Matthew presents the stripping of Jesus as taking place in isolation. They present it as part of other mistreatments in the *praetorium*. Other mistreatment includes striking Jesus, dressing him in purple or red clothing, spitting at him, and verbally insulting him. The purpose of this section is to investigate whether or not there might have been other violence, which is not listed, and whether this might have extended to sexual abuses.

As noted in Chapter 1, Mark and Matthew explicitly state that it was the whole cohort of soldiers (normally about 500 men) that was assembled for the 'mockery' of Jesus, most likely in the *praetorium* courtyard. Both Mark and Matthew mention that after dressing Jesus, the soldiers physically struck him with a rod (or reed) on his head. It is at least possible that some soldiers did not limit themselves to his head and targeted other exposed parts of his body, just as Sabrina Harman describes her colleague doing to the naked prisoner who reminded her of Jesus. Some soldiers might have struck or kicked against Jesus' exposed genitals as part of the mockery and striking.[10]

A difference between Mark and Matthew in their descriptions of the gathering of the soldiers is that Mark says 'and they called together the whole cohort' (Mark 15:16), using the verb *sugkaleō*, meaning 'to call together'. Matthew uses the verb *sunagō* and says, 'and they gathered the whole cohort around him' (Matt. 27:27). Matthew thereby confirms what is implied in Mark but not actually stated: the whole cohort was not only called but they responded and gathered. Furthermore, Matthew adds the specific detail *ep' auton*, which the NRSV translates as 'around him'. The language suggests close proximity, or even mobbing, rather than distance. The cohort are not merely spectators watching from a distance but are actively and intimately involved in the action.[11] The preposition *epi* is usually translated as 'upon' or 'on'. To translate it in this way here would certainly raise the possibility of sexual violence. Ulrich Luz says in his commentary: 'There, as Matthew states in exaggerated language, they turn loose "the entire cohort" on him' (Luz 2005, 513). Luz's reason for saying the language is exaggerated is unclear. He might assume that it was not the whole cohort, or he might doubt that the cohort would be let loose on a prisoner, or both.

The aforementioned assault on Muammar Gaddafi shows how quickly and easily sexual violence can happen when a helpless prisoner is surrounded by captors. In Gaddafi's case, the video footage suggests sexual assault took no more than seconds. If a whole cohort was assembled, with weapons to hand, it is conceivable that something similar happened in the melee that ensued.

Contemporary and ancient accounts suggest that 'making sport' of a captive to add to his humiliation and shame is a powerful motivation for sexualised torture (Tombs 2002b). In addition, if the soldiers were aware of Jesus' reputation as a religious teacher this might have added to their amusement (Tombs 2020a, 47–48). The soldiers in the *praetorium* might have believed that if a Jewish prisoner experienced a severe genital beating—or genital mutilation—this might have religious consequences on top of the physical harm inflicted. The prohibition on eunuchs in Deuteronomy 23:1 is phrased as 'No one whose testicles are crushed or whose penis is cut off shall be admitted to the assembly of the Lord'. Even though this is contradicted by Isaiah 56:3–5, it might have been an additional motivation for sexual cruelty against a Jewish prisoner.

Of course, if additional forms of sexualised violence or some form of sexual assault occurred in the *praetorium*, it would be simplistic to suppose that it could only have been penile rape, or even that penile rape would have been the most likely form of further assault. A number of other disturbing abuses would have been available to the soldiers.[12]

Whilst the opportunity to commit abuse is obvious, and it is clear that condemned prisoners sometimes suffered extreme mistreatment, the biblical texts do not allow definitive conclusions to be drawn. There are, however, at least two stories of mocking outside the gospels that merit further attention.

The Abuse of the Levite's Wife

The story of the Levite's wife (Judges 19) is described by biblical scholar Phyllis Trible as a 'text of terror' (Trible 1984).[13] It is not usually seen as a possible source for events in the *praetorium*, but the Greek used in the Septuagint translation of Judges 19 is interesting (Tombs 2021). There is no question that Judges 19 is a tale of extreme sexual violence. Trible notes that in describing the crime against the woman, the narrator repeats the same Hebrew word that was used for the men of the city wishing to 'know' the male guest.

> 'And they knew (*yd'*) her' (19:25c). In this context 'to know' loses all ambiguity. It means rape, and it parallels a verb connoting ruthless abuse. 'And they raped (*yd'*) her and tortured (*'ll*) her all night until the morning' (19:25d).
> (Trible 1984, 76)

As Trible notes, the Hebrew word *yada'* (*yd'*) is sexual in this context, even though the RSV translation that Trible uses has the potentially ambiguous or euphemistic 'knew'. The combination 'raped and tortured' presents the gang rape within a prolonged, intentional, and brutal mistreatment of the woman. It fits with a feminist analysis of rape as about power. The Hebrew word *'alal* (*'ll*) is usually translated into English as 'abused' (NRSV, RSV, KJV, NIV). In the Septuagint, *'alal* is translated by the Greek *empaizō*, which is then typically translated into English as 'mocked' or 'made fun of'. Trible's translation of *'alal* as 'tortured' rather than 'abused' or 'mocked' is unusual but appropriate. Trible's use of 'torture' underscores the severity of the abuse and mockery, and what she calls the 'extravagance' of the violence.

The Greek word *empaizō*, used for *'alal* in the Septuagint translation of Judges 19:25, is the same word used for mockery in Matthew 27:29 and 31. It also features in Matthew 20:19 when Jesus is on his way to Jerusalem and tells the 12 disciples that the Son of Man will be handed over to the Gentiles 'to be mocked and flogged and crucified'.

In the Bible, *empaizō* is used to express mockery of varying severity. For example, it can be used for mockery that is more jocular than threatening. In Luke 14:29, when Jesus warns 'otherwise, when he has laid a foundation and is not able to finish, all who see it will begin to ridicule him', the mockery seems primarily jocular and relatively harmless. In Matthew 27:41 the mockery is less jocular, but there is no suggestion of it involving physical abuse. The chief priests, the scribes and elders mock Jesus by challenging him to come down from the cross (Matt. 27:42–43). In Matthew 2:16, it might be translated as 'tricked': 'When Herod saw that he had been *tricked* by the wise men, he was infuriated, and he sent and killed all the children in and around Bethlehem who were two years old or under'. However, alongside these uses, the verb *empaizō* and its derivatives can also be used to cover torture and extreme physical violence. In Judges 19:25, the mockery clearly takes both a severe and sexual form. In 2 Maccabees 7:1–42 there is no explicit mention of sexual violence, but the seven sons are subjected to extreme torture and then put to death by Antiochus for their refusal to eat pork.[14] The torture includes whipping, burning, scalping, cutting out of the tongue, and cutting off hands and feet. This is referred to as 'sport' or 'mockery' (*empaizō*) in vv. 7 and 10.

In 1 Samuel 31:4, Saul voices his fear of the Philistines. He asks his armourbearer to kill him because he fears the Philistines will make 'sport of him' or 'mock him' if they capture him alive. Because Saul's armour bearer was too scared to do as Saul requested, Saul chose to take his own life. Whilst Saul's exact fears are not spelt out, and the language of 'make sport' may not seem threatening, the context suggests he had good reason to fear sexualised violence (Tombs 2014; Thiede 2022, 79–80). This fear would have been informed by his knowledge of how enemies were humiliated in defeat (Greenough 2021, 37). For example, Saul had previously demanded that David provide him with a dowry of 100 Philistine foreskins to marry Saul's daughter Michal (1 Sam. 18:26). David exceeded this request and presented Saul with 200 Philistine foreskins (1 Sam. 18:27). This is unlikely to have been forgiven or forgotten, and Saul would have had good reason to fear vengeance. Furthermore, as Barbara Thiede explains, the language is more suggestive of sexualised violence than most translations reveal:

> Translations suggest the Philistines will insult Saul ('make sport of'), but the Hebrew is more graphic. The verse includes the hitpa'el form of *alal* . . . coupled with the prefix *bet* . . . a combination that indicates sexual violence. The phrasing used here, *v'hital'lu bi*, is found in Judges 19:25, when the Levite's *pilegesh* is taken and gang raped by a mob of men. The men raped her and, as most translations render the phrase, 'abused her' all night long.

In a footnote to this, Thiede draws attention to the contrast in how translators deal with the two passages:

> Translators use sexually graphic words like 'abuse' or 'rape' about the *pilegesh* but offer different language ('make sport of') when the same Hebrew expression is used about the abuse of male characters.[15]

Understanding that Saul fears sexualised violence from the Philistines helps makes sense of what happened after Saul's death. The Philistines find Saul's body and the bodies of his sons the next day. They cut off Saul's head, strip Saul of his armour, and fasten his body to the wall of Beth-shan (1 Sam. 31:9–10). These details may be understated and leave open the possibility of additional humiliations of the corpse. For example, Saul's body might have been impaled on the wall in a manner suggestive of sexual violation. In any case, the public disgrace of Saul's body on the wall was so great that when the men of Jabesh Gilead learn of it they are stirred into action. They rescue the bodies of Saul and his sons from the wall, take them back to Jabesh, burn them, and then bury the bones (1 Sam. 31:11–13).

To sum up, biblical texts refer to sexualised violence against men in ways that are indirect and might not even be noticed. The Hebrew touches upon Saul's fears euphemistically, and the English translation then makes the scene even more benign. Thus the use of *empaizō* in Matthew 27:26–31 may be more suggestive of sexual violence than first appears. It may offer a quiet clue that the mistreatment in the *praetorium* can be read as an understated account of further mistreatment that echoes back to both the rape of the *pilegesh* in Judges 19:25 and the fears of Saul in 1 Samuel 31:4.

The possibility of the further mistreatment of Jesus becomes even more plausible when his experience in the *praetorium* is viewed alongside another example of soldier mockery, recorded by Josephus, about ten years after Jesus' crucifixion.

The Death of Herod Agrippa

In book 19 of *Antiquities*, the Jewish historian Josephus describes the outrageous behaviour of soldiers in 44 CE after the death of Herod Agrippa. Agrippa, who was a grandson of Herod the Great, ruled over Judea and Samaria from 41 to 44 CE. Josephus records the reactions amongst the non-Jewish populace of Caesarea and Sebaste to Agrippa's death:

> But when it became known that Agrippa had departed this life, the people of Caesarea and of Sebaste, forgetting his benefactions, behaved in the most hostile fashion. They hurled insults, too foul to be mentioned, at the deceased; and all who were then on military service—and they were a considerable number—went off to their homes, and seizing the images of the king's daughters carried them with one accord to the brothels, where they set them

up on the roofs and offered them every possible sort of insult, doing things too indecent to be reported.

(Josephus, *Antiquities*, 19:356–357)

The text describes how soldiers from Caesarea and Sebaste showed their hostility towards Agrippa through outrageous public insults directed at his three young daughters, Berenice (aged 16), Mariamme (aged 10) and Drusilla (aged 6). The images (or statues) of the daughters were placed up on the roofs of brothels and then offered 'every possible sort of insult'. The precise nature of the insults is not detailed, however, the placement of the images above brothels (*porneia*) makes clear the sexual dimension. The sexual insults offered to the images were a way to insult the daughters, and thereby a way to insult the deceased Agrippa.

Furthermore, Josephus makes clear that he has deliberately refrained from giving the full story. He goes as far as to state that some of the mockery was 'too indecent to be reported'. The reader is left to guess at what else might have happened, but is guided by the term 'indecent' (*aschēmonestera*), which suggests a sexual dimension.

The mocking behaviour of soldiers immediately following the death of a King of the Jews in 44 CE has relevance for the mocking behaviour of soldiers just prior to the death of Jesus as King of the Jews (usually dated c. 30–33 CE). The soldiers living in Caesarea and Sebaste who mocked Agrippa were most likely locally recruited Roman auxiliaries.[16] Caesarea was on the coast (and served as the usual residence of the Roman governor), whilst Sebaste was in Samaria. Both cities had large non-Jewish populations and a history of conflict with their Jewish neighbours in the towns.

Prior to the Jewish War (66–70 CE) Roman forces in Judea appear to have been constituted almost entirely by auxiliary forces, and the non-Jewish populations of these cities provided most of the auxiliaries who were recruited into the Roman army (Zeichmann 2018). Thus 'the soldiers of the governor' in Matthew 27:27 were most probably locally recruited auxiliaries from Caesarea and Sebaste. When the opportunity arises, these local auxiliaries made their contempt for a King of the Jews as clear as they possibly could. Indecent and unspeakable acts, including some form of performative sexual violence, are central to the mockery of Agrippa and could have been part of the mockery of Jesus.

Agrippa was a powerful local ruler. He commanded a significant territory and was in alliance with Rome. If such a powerful figure was subjected to mockery, there is no reason to suppose that the soldiers would have held back from insulting and sexualised mockery of Jesus. The fact that such indecency and torture is not explicitly recorded in the gospels does not prove it did not happen. As Josephus says, some things are too indecent to be recorded.

Conclusion

Many commentaries treat the scene of the mocking in the *praetorium* more like infantile horseplay rather than a deeply troubling display of power. We do not know what happened in the *praetorium*. However, if the gospel narratives are read more carefully in light of torture practices past and present, there are troubling possibilities. Namely, there may be silence about violence that was considered 'too indecent to be recorded'.

Notes

1 'For example, in the International Criminal Tribunal for the former Yugoslavia (ICTY) case *The Prosecutor v. Ranko Češić*, Presiding Judge Alphons Orie expressly rejected the defence's argument that proof of the perpetrator's intent to 'satisfy any sexual feelings' is an element of the crime of rape. There is no reason why his position would not apply *mutatis mutandis* to any sexual violence crime (WIGJ 2019, 25 n. 13).
2 On gang rape as an instrument of male social bonding and affirmation of masculine identity, see Thiede (2022).
3 See especially Deacy and Pierce (1997) and Reeder (2017). On Roman attitudes to sexuality more widely, see Langlands (2006), Hallett and Skinner (1997), and Williams (2010). On sexual violence in the Hebrew Bible see, for example, Trible (1984), Nidditch (1993), Stone (1996), Lemos (2006), Blyth et al. (2018), Winkler (2020), Melanchthon and Whitaker (2021), and Thiede (2022).
4 The rape of an enslaved person belonging to another citizen might be punished, not as protection to the slave but on the basis of damage done to the other citizen's 'property'.
5 On racialised aspects of rape and colonial legacies, see Gqola (2015, 37–53).
6 The battle at the Eurymedon River in c. 466 BCE during the wars between Greece and Persia offers a compelling connection between military conquest and sexual violence from an earlier period. Kenneth Dover discusses the red Attic vase (the so-called Eurymedon wine jug from c. 460 BCE) which depicts the explicit association between male rape and military conquest. On one side, a man is shown striding aggressively forward. He is naked except for a cloak, and stretches one hand out as if to grab something whilst grasping his erect penis in his other hand. On the other side of the jug, a man in Persian clothing bends forward at the hips and twists his upper body to face the viewer. He holds his hands up as if surrendering. An inscription reads 'I am Eurymedon, I stand bent forward'. Dover explains, 'This expresses the exultation of the "manly" Athenians at their victory over the "womanish" Persians' (Dover 1978, 105). Although the vase is Greek rather than Roman, it suggests how and why male rape of a captive would have been in keeping with the attributes of Roman virility described by Williams (2010). See also Trexler (1995, 14–23).
7 For example, two passages in Plato connect castration and torture to a form of execution which the Loeb translators refer to as 'crucifixions' but the details are not entirely clear. In *The Republic*, Plato refers to various punishments which might be inflicted before a 'crucifixion': these include branding irons on the eyes and other extreme forms of suffering (*Republic* 362a). In the *Gorgias*, Plato lists as punishment for a man who would make himself a despot as being 'put on the rack and castrated and have his eyes burnt out, and after suffering himself, and seeing inflicted on his wife and children, a number of grievous torments of every kind, he be finally crucified or burnt in a coat of pitch' (*Gorgias*, 473c). See Chapter 3 on why the Greek terminology for crucifixion is hard to interpret.
8 Cited Coleman (1990, 60). Coleman asks what sort of coercion might be required to persuade a prisoner to do this. She speculates that it most likely would have been used as a mitigated sentence. 'If the Romans conceived of self-castration as a mitigated sentence, it seems probable that it was as an alternative to a related form of execution: a likely candidate is that mode of crucifixion, mentioned by Seneca, whereby the victim

was impaled through the genitals' (p. 61). This passage from Seneca (*Dialogues*, 6.20.3) will be discussed in the next chapter.

9 The version of events that the Levite gives to the assembled tribes in Judges 19 offers an example of such reticence. He tells them that the Benjaminites in Gibeah threatened him with death, but he makes no mention of the fact that they threatened him with rape. Likewise, as noted above, it is implied that the Lorcian townsmen (not just the women and children) experienced 'unspeakable abuses' (Livy, *History of Rome*, 29.8.8), but when the Lorcian delegation reported to the Senate in Rome on what happened, they spoke of abuses against women and children, but any abuses against their own bodies were left unspoken: 'They are all robbing, pillaging, assaulting, wounding, killing; they are raping married women, girls, and freeborn boys torn from their parents' arms. Every day our city is being captured, every day pillaged. Day and night all of it rings with the wailing of women and boys being violated and carried off' (Livy, *History of Rome*, 29.17.15–16).

10 See the image 'Geisselung Christi' (The Flagellation of Christ) (1538) by Lucas Cranach the Elder: https://commons.wikimedia.org/wiki/File:Lucas_Cranach_d._Ä._087.jpg.

11 An alternative translation might be 'gathered against him' (see Acts 4.26–27). See 'the kings of the earth took their stand, and the rulers have gathered together against the Lord and against his Messiah' (Acts 4.26) and 'for in this city, in fact, both Herod and Pontius Pilate, with the gentiles and the peoples of Israel, gathered together against your holy servant Jesus, whom you anointed' (Acts 4.27). The preposition seems to be used in this way in Matthew 22.34, where the Pharisees are reported as gathering 'against' Jesus, even though Jesus is not present.

12 Williams (2010, 197–203) explains that the social stigma of effeminacy was even stronger for men who were forced to fellate another male. Since the identity of the active or penetrative partner is less clear in oral sex—it might seem to be the one who fellates rather than the one who is fellated—the Romans had the term *irrumation*, which does not have an equivalent in English. This term refers to the one who is fellated and makes him the active subject as the one who penetrates the mouth. This preserves the important Roman principle that a Roman man should always be the active penetrator and not the passive penetrated. There is evidence that *irrumation* was an even more shameful form of penetration than anal rape, and it may have been reserved for adult men, whereas anal rape was more associated with boys.

13 The Hebrew term *pilegesh* is used, which is often translated as 'concubine' but might be better understood as a wife without full status. For simplicity, she will be described here simply as 'wife'.

14 Their mother is also put to death, but the text does not record if she was also tortured (2 Macc. 7:41).

15 Thiede (2022, 94 n. 19).

16 Josephus (*War*, 2.268) suggests that, at least while Felix was procurator (52–60 CE), the Roman garrison in Caesarea was locally recruited auxiliaries.

3 Crucifixion

And they crucified him.

(Mark 15:24)

And when they had crucified him . . .

(Matt. 27:35)

They crucified him.

(Luke 23:33)

There they crucified him.

(John 19:18)

Introduction

Unlike the events in the *praetorium*, which took place behind closed doors, crucifixions took place in full public view. Indeed, the public spectacle of violence was part of their purpose (Kyle 1998). They were intended not only to punish and degrade the immediate victim but to deter and terrify onlookers and everyone else.

Individual degradation and public terror provide a context for the examination in this chapter of the possibility that Roman crucifixions might have sometimes involved penetrative sexualised violence. Given how the crucifixion is usually represented in Christian art, this suggestion may seem shocking and implausible. Before proceeding, it is therefore appropriate to repeat a content warning: the possibility of sexualised violence explored in this chapter is especially confronting. Some readers may therefore prefer to skip or defer this chapter. The material is challenging and difficult to interpret. What I outline below is intended as a prompt for justifying a more thorough investigation on this sensitive but urgent topic. If the evidence is persuasive, I hope this chapter will encourage additional careful and contextualised reading towards further work of this kind.

Following the pattern set in previous chapters, first I will examine examples of torture practices in recent times which might shed light on the issues discussed in the sections that follow. The example is especially disturbing and will be kept brief.

DOI: 10.4324/9780429289750-4

The chapter then examines the conventional representation of Jesus' crucifixion in art and contrasts this with the details in the gospel accounts. It suggests that the picture that most people have of Jesus' crucifixion—and of crucifixion in general—rests more on Christian art than the sparse details in biblical texts. All the gospels (Mark 15:24; Matt. 27:35; Luke 23:33; John 19:18) report that Jesus was crucified. However, none gives much detail on what this involved. There are many details that remain unspecified and unclear.

The chapter continues by exploring the historical development of Roman crucifixion with particular attention to earlier impalement practices. It describes ancient impalement punishments, as documented most clearly in the Assyrian Empire of the ninth to seventh centuries BCE (the use of 'longitudinal impalement' and 'transversal impalement'). It then turns to public suspension executions practised by the Persians, Greeks, and Carthaginians. These can be seen as steps in the historical transition from earlier impalement punishments to Roman crucifixion. These suspension executions nailed or tied the victim to stakes or poles or other structures. They were an even more effective instrument of terror because they extended the experience of shame and prolonged the agony of death. Recent work has prompted a debate about how these pre-Roman suspension executions were conducted, and whether or not it is helpful to refer to them as 'crucifixions'.

In the Roman period, a clearer picture of crucifixion emerges. Roman crucifixions can be seen as a further refinement of previous suspension executions and undertaken for the same purpose of increasing the effectiveness of public execution as an instrument of state terror. References in historical sources to features like the crossbeam and nails provide important evidence for how the conventional depiction of the crucifixion of Jesus in art came to be conceptualised. Even so, the historical sources are not clear or detailed. The historical evidence is hard to interpret; any conclusions need to be more tentative than the conventional artistic image of crucifixion suggests.

Questions that require particular attention include whether or not impalement persisted alongside crucifixion in Roman times, and whether it might have been incorporated in crucifixion in some way. An initial attempt at examining evidence of impalement in Roman crucifixions is the focus of the next section. Three passages in Seneca the Younger (4 BCE–65 CE) suggest Roman crucifixion did not fully displace impalement. These deserve further investigation.

The final part of the chapter turns to the evidence that relates more directly to Jesus. Here we consider a specific passage by the second-century Christian writer Justin Martyr. In this passage Justin connects Jesus to the sacrificial Passover lamb known as the 'Paschal lamb'. Justin's suggestion that Jesus be seen as the Paschal lamb is hardly an original idea. It builds on Paul's writing (1 Cor. 5:7) and the narrative presentation in John 19 that makes parallels between Jesus' death and the sacrifice of the Paschal lamb (Brown 1994, 1076–1078). However, Justin's words appear to suggest that part of the similarity is to be found in the impalement of the lamb on a skewer or spit. This raises the question of whether Justin believed that impalement might also have been part of Jesus' experience in crucifixion. Although it is not possible to answer this question with certainty, these ancient sources raise questions. The passage from Justin and the three passages from Seneca, two ancient sources (albeit not eyewitnesses to the crucifixion), suggest the need for further research.

The Stick

Muammar Gaddafi was the authoritarian head of state in Libya for over 40 years (1969–2011). Towards the end of his rule, as he faced growing challenges, he was accused of authorising sexual violence against opponents to his regime. In 2011, a rebellion against him finally forced him to flee, but he was quickly hunted down. As described in Chapter 2, on 20 October 2011 Gaddafi was captured and killed. Before he was killed, he was subjected to sexual assault with a bayonet. Many of his supporters were subsequently imprisoned and subjected to torture.

In 2017, the journalist Cécile Allegra interviewed a Tunis-based human rights group for the French periodical *Le Monde*. In an article shared with *The Guardian*—and published with a warning about the graphic information included—Allegra detailed the experiences of Gaddafi supporters imprisoned by those who had previously suffered under Gaddafi's regime. The prisoners reported being threatened or violated in different ways. Allegra describes a video she saw of a prisoner having his trousers and underwear pulled down, and then a rocket launcher being placed up against his naked buttocks. Here threat, humiliation, and suggestion of penetrative sexualised violence are evident to the degree that they are indistinguishable.

Another detainee described a torture known as 'the wheel': he was stripped and 'folded-double' (bent over with his knees pressed against his chest) and then pushed into the middle of a tyre that was hanging from the ceiling. Constrained in the tyre in this way—with his buttocks protruding and exposed from the centre of the tyre—it was easy for guards to penetrate the prisoner with any weapons or instruments they might wish to use (Allegra 2017).

Alongside 'the wheel' the same prisoner reported being subjected to 'the stick'. This time a broom handle was fixed on a wall just below waist height and prisoners were forced to bend over and self-penetrate themselves against the stick. One detainee reported, 'If you want to eat, you have to take off your pants, back on to the broom and not move off until the jailer sees blood flowing. Nobody can escape it' (Allegra 2017). According to Allegra's report, there were dozens of documented cases and each one reported a similar form of assault in detention, the majority of these featuring sexualised degradation.

The Cross

As a form of execution, crucifixion combined pain, shame, and death. When ancient writers mention crucifixion, an emotional intensity is conveyed in the use of superlatives. Cicero says that crucifixion is a 'most cruel and disgusting penalty' (*Against Verres*, 2.5.165). Likewise, the Jewish historian Josephus also uses a superlative to express his feelings on crucifixion when he calls it 'the most pitiable of deaths' (*Jewish War*, 7.203).

Cicero's view that there is something 'unspeakable' about crucifixion—at least when it is inflicted on a Roman citizen—appears in the speech he prepared in defence of Gaius Rabirius. He says:

> The very word 'cross' should be far removed not only from the person of a Roman citizen but from his thoughts, his eyes and his ears. For it is not only the actual occurrence of these things or the endurance of them, but liability to them, the expectation, nay, the mere mention of them, that is unworthy of a Roman citizen and a free man.
>
> (*Orations*, 'Speech in Defence of Gaius Rabirius', 16)

When Cicero describes the crucifixion ordered by Verres of the Roman citizen Gavius (during the time Verres served as magistrate of Sicily, 73–70 BCE) he appears almost lost for words. He writes: 'To bind a Roman citizen is a crime, to flog him is an abomination, to slay him is almost an act of murder: to crucify him is—what? There is no fitting word that can possibly describe so horrible a deed' (*Against Verres* 2.5.170). Here again, Cicero's outrage is not so much about crucifixion *per se*, but that Gavius was a Roman citizen and yet Verres treated him as slave or foreigner. In doing so, 'you declared war upon the whole principle of the rights of the Roman citizen body. You were the enemy, I say again, not of that individual man, but of the common liberties of us all' (*Against Verres* 2.5.169).

When the Romans first adopted crucifixion, it was used primarily to humiliate and punish slaves, but it did not always involve death. Slaves had economic value, and crucifixion was a severe punishment but could be used in ways that stopped short of killing them.[1] Slaves could survive to continue to work.

It was probably from the first century BCE onwards that the Romans started to use crucifixion as an aggravated form of execution referred to by the euphemism 'slaves' punishment' (*supplicium servile*; Valerius Maximus, *Memorable Doings and Sayings*, 8.4.1). Over time, the 'slaves' punishment' was extended as a form of execution to anyone who rebelled against Roman authority. This included bandits and insurgents.

The infliction of shame remained integral to crucifixion. Cicero refers to the cross as a 'tree of shame' (*Orations*, 'Speech in Defence of Gaius Rabirius', 13). Likewise, in Justin Martyr's dialogue with Trypho, Trypho refers to 'a shameful and dishonourable death, cursed by the law' (Justin, *Dialogue* 90.1).[2] Because of the association of crucifixion with slavery and disgrace, it was very rare for crucifixion to be used against Roman citizens, but there were some cases where treason was involved (Hengel 1977, 39–45). Usually, the emphasis on the inviolability of the body of Roman citizens offered Romans a protection that others in the Empire did not have.

By contrast, in the provinces, crucifixion was a brutally effective means to remind conquered subjects of the cost of opposition to Rome. It was an instrument of 'state terror' through public torture (Tombs 1999). Cicero speaks of those who 'hang on the cross' as experiencing 'the worst extreme of the tortures inflicted upon slaves' (*Against Verres* 2.5.169). The impact of this public spectacle went well beyond the punishment of the immediate victim. It sent a visceral message to the wider public about the consequences of opposition to Rome. Mass crucifixions of insurgents served as an especially frightful warning on the harsh consequences that could be expected by those who chose to resist. For example, Josephus describes how in 4 BCE Varus (Governor of Syria) responded to the upheaval caused by the inept rule of Herod's son Archelaus by crucifying 2,000 'ringleaders' of the troubles (*Jewish War* 2.69–79).[3]

There are a wide range of references to crucifixion in Roman sources, but the details on what precisely crucifixion involved are left vague. The reticence on details in the gospels is in keeping with this wider pattern. Josephus records many crucifixions, but in most cases he gives scant details. For example, Josephus offers nothing directly on Jesus' crucifixion beyond reporting that it happened under Pilate. He says only that when Pilate heard high-standing Jews were accusing Jesus, Pilate condemned Jesus to be crucified (*Ant.* 18.63). In a description that Josephus gives of crucifixions ordered by Titus during the siege of Jerusalem, he describes 500 or even more Jewish captives being captured daily. After scourging and being 'subjected to torture of every description', the prisoners were crucified opposite the city walls (*Jewish War*, 5.450). There is a reference that is intriguing—and telling in its lack of specificity—in what he describes as 'amusement' in these mass crucifixions. Josephus writes:

> The soldiers out of rage and hatred amused themselves by nailing their prisoners in different postures; and so great was their number, that space could not be found for the crosses nor crosses for the bodies.
> (*Jewish War*, 5.451)

Some Roman sources are notable for their silence. Gerald O'Collins (1992, 1208) points out that Tacitus does not even mention the innumerable crucifixions during the Jewish War that Josephus recorded (Tacitus, *Histories*, 5.8.13). The brief mention that Tacitus makes to Jesus' crucifixion says he was one who 'suffered the extreme penalty under Pontius Pilate during the reign of Tiberius' (*Annals*, 15.44). 'Extreme penalty' (*supplicio adfectus*) is an alternative euphemism for crucifixion, which like the term 'slaves' punishment' stops just short of using the dreaded word.

One consequence of the reticence in the Roman writings is that the fullest narrative account in ancient literature that recounts Jesus' trial, flogging, and crucifixion is left to the gospels. Yet even in the gospel accounts, which centre on the story of the life, ministry, and death of Jesus, many details about crucifixion are unclear. When it comes to the act of crucifixion itself, the gospels are almost as terse as the non-biblical sources.[4] At the time, contemporaries may have filled in these details of customary practice from what they knew or had seen, so the lack of written detail was not such a deficiency.

Depictions of Jesus on the cross only started to appear in Christian art considerably later, beginning in the fifth century CE.[5] These depictions follow a fairly consistent set of conventions. Readers today are likely to be so familiar with these conventions that the lack of detail in the ancient texts might not be noticed. Instead, gaps in the text are easily filled with assumptions gained from ubiquitous images of Jesus' crucifixion.

The conventional artistic image of Jesus' crucifixion invariably features the so-called Latin cross, as shown for example in the painting 'Crucifixion' by Rembrandt (1631).[6] The Latin cross comprises two wooden beams, a longer upright (*stipes*) with a shorter crossbeam (*patibulum*). The crossbeam is fixed a little way down from the top of the upright. In the sixteenth century, the Humanist scholar Justus Lipsius (1547–1606) provided terminology for different forms of the cross, which remains helpful today. Lipsius drew a distinction, for instance, between the *crux simplex* and the *crux compacta*. The conventional Latin cross is an example of a *crux compacta*, comprising two pieces joined together. By contrast, the *crux simplex* was a single upright beam or stake that stood on its own.

Within these two categories Lipsius drew some further helpful subdivisions. Hence, for a *crux simplex* he contrasted the *crux simplex ad affixionem* with the *crux simplex ad infixionem* (Lipsius 1606). The condemned was fastened (or 'affixed') to the *crux simplex ad affixionem* with ropes or nails and left suspended. The *crux simplex ad infixionem*, on the other hand, involved impalement of the victim on the upright. For mass crucifixions, or to crucify someone quickly, a *crux simplex ad affixionem* might be used. However, for individual crucifixions, or small group crucifixions, crucifixion on a two-piece *crux compacta* was more likely, especially when the purpose was to make a prolonged public spectacle of the punishment. Within the category of *crux compacta*, Lipsius also distinguished between the *crux immissa* (†) and the *crux commissa* (T).[7]

The *crux commissa* (T) is often called a Tau cross because it resembles the Greek letter *tau* in upper case form. The design would have been more stable, convenient, and probably more widely used than the Latin cross. One advantage was that if the condemned carried only the crossbeam to the place of crucifixion, which seems to have been the practice, then making a Tau cross would have been easier and more stable than the construction of a Latin cross. The crossbeam for the Tau cross could be placed on top of the upright—resting securely in a prepared groove—rather than needing to be affixed by rope or nails against the front of the upright, as required by a Latin cross. The Epistle of Barnabas (a non-canonical gospel, probably written in the late first or early second century) implies an upper case *tau* shape for the cross.[8] However, in Christian art it is the Latin cross, with the crossbeam attached beneath the top of the upright, that is usually depicted, and the Tau cross is less common.[9]

In early art Jesus was usually shown on the cross with his arms outstretched horizontally along the crossbeam and his body matching the shape of the cross. In later art, it became more usual to show him as hanging down from the crossbeam with his body in a Y shape. His hands or wrists are usually shown as either nailed or tied to the crossbeam.[10] His legs typically hang down vertically in line with the upright. They are usually shown as secured to the upright, often with one foot placed in front of the other and secured with a single nail through the feet. On the upright which extends above the head of Jesus, a small wooden board (*titulus*) is usually shown, with Pilate's words.[11] Some crosses depict Jesus as standing on a small platform or stand (*suppedaneum*) fixed to the lower part of the upright.[12]

One feature that is rarely included in Christian art, but which is mentioned in early Christian writings and is important for this chapter, is the *sedile*. This was an attachment or modification on the upright on which the victim might sit or perch. Irenaeus, Bishop of Lyon in the second century, writes, 'The very form of the cross, too, has five end points, two in length, two in breadth, and one in the middle, on which the person rests who is fixed by the nails' (*Adversus Haereses*, II.24.4). Justin Martyr writes, 'And the part which is fixed in the centre, on which are suspended those who are crucified, also stands out like a horn' (*Dialogue with Trypho*, § 91). Justin's description suggests that the *sedile* was more like a peg than a ledge or platform.

The conventional picture of Jesus with arms outstretched and nailed to a Latin cross has become so well established and familiar that most readers are likely to be unaware that this depiction is sourced from disparate evidence outside the gospels. Even most Christians are likely to be unaware that their understanding of Jesus' crucifixion depends more on art than on the gospel text or historical sources. In most cases, the conventional image is so strongly impressed in the imagination that it seamlessly fills in the details that the texts themselves leave out. A careful reading of the texts shows that limiting what is known to only what is explicitly attested in the biblical texts gives a much less vivid image when compared to that conventionally represented in art.

There are, of course, four gospel crucifixion narratives, not just one, and each gospel narrative has its own distinctive features. Nonetheless, there is enough in common among them to attempt a basic outline, drawing attention to variations, rather than to discuss each version separately in turn.

After the mockery in the *praetorium*, Jesus is re-dressed and led out of the city to be crucified. For this journey, the cross is either given to Simon of Cyrene to carry (Mark 15:21, Matt. 27:32, and Luke 23:26) or Jesus is forced to carry his cross himself (John 19:17). Most depictions in art show Jesus rather than Simon of Cyrene carrying the cross, and the cross he carries is almost always shown as a full two-piece Latin cross, with the crossbeam already attached. At Golgotha, an Aramaic name meaning 'the place of the skull' (Matt. 27:33; Mark 15:22; Luke 23:33; John 19:17), Jesus is stripped a final time and then crucified.

Two other men are crucified alongside Jesus, one to his right and one to his left (Matt. 27:44; Mark 15:27; Luke 23:32; John 19:18). Mark 15:29 records the taunting Jesus was subjected to by the crowd. All the gospels record that Jesus spoke from the cross and was offered something to drink, though the details and the sequence vary. Mark records Jesus initially being offered wine mixed with myrrh (15:23), and then after he cried out, he was also offered sour wine (15:36). Matthew makes no mention of the wine and myrrh but says that after Jesus cried out, he was offered sour wine (Matt. 27:48). Luke says that sour wine was offered

(23:36) but places Jesus' cry from the cross a bit after rather than before the wine (23:46). John 19:28–30 states that Jesus said he was thirsty, and he was offered sour wine, and when he had received it, he said 'it is finished' and died.

Each gospel also records the presence of women, but here too the details vary. Mark 15:40 and Matthew 27:55 say that were many women who looked on from a distance, and among them was Mary Magdalene. Luke 23:27 says that women accompanied Jesus on his way to Golgotha but does not record names. John 19:25 places Mary the mother of Jesus, Mary Magdalene, and two other women near the cross.[13]

Having four separate accounts, broadly in agreement, might be expected to give us a good basis for reconstructing how Jesus was crucified. But this is not the case. All versions speak of *where* Jesus was crucified (and give the place as Golgotha) and give information on *who* was present and *what* was said. However, none of them gives much information on *how* he was crucified. As with the other ancient sources, the gospels supply minimal information on the mechanics of crucifixion as a form of execution. What *can* be gleaned is that Jesus was affixed to some kind of 'cross', that his death took some time but came more quickly than was often the case, and that Jesus died before the two criminals crucified to either side of him. That is it.

Readers of the text might not notice how sparse the account is. Instead, as we have discussed, details of the crucifixion scene are readily imagined, not least because of representations in Christian art. But *in the text* there is no information about how the cross was constructed or how Jesus was affixed to it. Abundant images show Jesus' arms nailed or tied to a crossbeam, but there is no specific mention of a crossbeam in the gospels or elsewhere. The crossbeam is *read into* the pictorial scene on account of what is believed about Roman customs or otherwise assumed.[14] But only contextual information from outside the gospels makes any case for a crossbeam plausible. Likewise, none of the gospels makes any explicit mention of nails or nailing at Golgotha. Evidence for the nails is offered in the resurrection narratives but not in the crucifixion narratives.[15]

The little evidence available from archaeological sources confirms that nailing through the ankles was used in at least some crucifixions. One source for this practice is the bones discovered by Vassilios Tzaferis at Givat ha-Mivtar in 1968 (Tzaferis 1985).[16] These bones are believed to be from a first-century victim of crucifixion called Yehohanan, the son of Hagakol. Tzaferis argues that it was likely that Yehohanan was nailed to the cross with his legs in a bent double position and his knees positioned to the left side, forcing him to twist his body from the waist up into a forced and unnatural position, supported by a *sedile* wood block under his left buttock.[17]

Displaying the cross in public maximised the victim's humiliation, and the shame was seen in readily gendered ways of unmanly vulnerability (Moore and Anderson 2003; Conway 2008; Asikainen 2018; Stratton 2019). For Jews, the shame was further exacerbated, because 'anyone hung on a tree is under a curse' (Deut. 21:23). Paul refers to this belief in relation to Jesus' crucifixion (Gal. 3:13). The vulnerable body might suffer further violence if it attracted carrion birds either before or after death when allowed to hang unprotected. Reference to this possibility is made in Genesis 40, where the baker imprisoned with Joseph recounts his dream. In the dream the baker has three baskets of baked goods on his head and birds eat from the top basket meant for Pharaoh (Gen. 40:16–17). Joseph's interpretation of the dream is that 'within three days Pharaoh will lift up your head—from you!—and hang you on a pole; and the birds will eat the flesh from you' (Gen. 40:19), and the denouement to the story confirms Joseph's interpretation. Josephus says that 'he [Joseph] told him that the baskets meant three days, and that on the third day he would be crucified and devoured by birds, being unable to defend himself' (*Jewish Antiquities* 2.72). Crucifixion could therefore involve attacks on the corpse—or even, on the still-living body—by carrion birds.[18] Since Jesus was crucified on the eve of the Sabbath, this would have added to the sense of urgency that prompted Jesus' followers to take his body down from the cross and not leave him exposed until Sunday (Mark 15:42–43).

To sum up, whilst the conventional image of crucifixion is richly detailed, information about the cross is very limited in the biblical texts. There is minimal information in the text on the form of the cross and only partial information on how Jesus was affixed to it. Most readers unconsciously draw on Christian art to fill in the gaps. Filling in the text in this way is so instinctive that most readers are barely aware of it. But are the details supplied by conventional images accurate regarding first-century crucifixion in Judea? Does Christian art facilitate or obscure a fair reading of the gospel text?

To illustrate challenges to the dominant conventional depictions, I turn to three images from the second and third centuries: the Puteoli graffito, the Pereire magical gem (Figure 1), and the Palatine graffito.

The second-century Puteoli graffito was discovered in Puteoli (modern Pozzuoli), a port town to the south of Rome (Cook 2014, 203–204).[19] A graffito is a scratching on a wall, and in this case the image is accompanied by an inscription. It was found on an inner wall in the room of a tavern near the amphitheatre. There is no reason to think it is intended to depict Jesus. Nonetheless it is significant because it appears to be the earliest known detailed visual image of a crucifixion. The art historian Felicity Harley-McGowan (2019a, 107–108) suggests a date as early as 100–130 CE, based on features of wall painting and on inscriptions alongside which the graffito appears and which are associated with the time of either Hadrian or Trajan. The graffito shows a figure crucified on a T-shaped cross with arms outstretched and secured to a crossbeam. The figure is shown from behind with head turned to the right. The broad shoulders and slimmer hips suggest a male. The legs are bowed outwards but the ankles are secured to the upright.[20] Curved horizontal lines run across the body, as if the figure was flogged or perhaps even flayed. His mouth is open, which might suggest suffocating or screaming. The upright of the cross narrows and then widens again quite notably about halfway up.

The Pereire gem (Figure 1) is slightly later, and is usually dated to the late second century or early third century CE. It is a mottled green and brown jasper gemstone once owned by Roger Pereire and now in the British Museum. This gemstone is likely to have been used as a magic amulet for warding off evil

Figure 1 Magical gem, British Museum

spirits and is sometimes referred to as the 'Magic Crucifixion' gem (Kotansky 2017; Harley-McGowan 2019a, 2019b). It is probable that the owner was a non-Christian who wished to appropriate some of the magical power of the cross, since magic gems were prohibited for Christians. It presents a bearded naked figure shown from in front, on a Tau shaped cross, with wrists tied to crossbeam. The figure is male and has an erect penis. The upright of the cross seems to narrow as it contacts his body.

Harley-McGowan (2019a, 106) describes the image and its inscription:

> Written around the image, a nine-line inscription begins above the victim's head with what may be interpreted as 'Son, Father, Jesus Christ'—hence the identification of the figure as Jesus. This title is followed by uncertain magical names, vowels, and possibly the words 'hung up'. On the reverse, names familiar from other magical texts are present, as is the name Emmanuel—the Hebrew 'God is with us', taken by Christians to be a reference to Jesus prophesied in Isaiah 7:14–16.

Because of this inscription the gem is one of the very earliest depictions of a crucifixion which identifies the victim as Jesus.

The Palatine graffito is also probably from the late second or early third century CE (Harley-McGowan 2019b). It was discovered at the Palatine Palace in Rome, in a room that was excavated in 1856 and believed to have been living quarters for enslaved people. It is now on display in the Palatine Antiquarium.[21] Like the Puteoli graffito, it shows a crucified figure from behind. The figure stands upright with arms outstretched beneath the crossbeam of a T-shaped cross.

The hands or wrists are nailed or tied tightly to the crossbeam, and the figure is standing straight-legged on a *suppendaeum*. The feet are not secured to the upright or to each other, and they seem to be resting freely on the *suppendaeum*. The head is drawn as a donkey's head, which might reflect the rumour that Christians worshipped a donkey-headed god—an accusation known to Minucius Felix (*Octavius*, 9.3 and 28.7) and Tertullian (*Apologeticus*, 16.12). He appears to be wearing a sleeveless tunic on his upper body which ends just above the buttocks. It is possible that the garment is a skin and attached to the donkey's head.[22]

Another figure is shown to the left of the scene looking up at the cross. An inscription in Greek capitals over four lines reads: 'Alexamenos worships his God'. The figure to the left is therefore usually identified as Alexamenos and believed to be an enslaved Christian. The scene is interpreted as an anti-Christian caricature which scoffs at the foolishness of Alexamenos and his veneration of a crucified God. The figure on the cross is not explicitly identified, but because of reference to worship and God in the inscription the graffito appears to be mocking both the enslaved Christian and the crucified Christ.

These three images support some of the significant elements in the conventional image of Jesus' crucifixion while also suggesting, or allowing for, significant differences. In support, they show a figure who is vertically suspended or affixed on a two-piece cross. The arms are outstretched on the crossbeam and nailed or tied at the hands or wrists. However, the differences with the conventional image are also important.

First, all three show a T-shaped cross rather than a Latin cross. As discussed above, there is reason to believe that a Tau cross would have had practical benefits and been more common.

Second, none of these images suggests the crucified figure is wearing a loincloth. In the Puteoli graffito the figure is not wearing any clothing. If the parallel marks on the body are from scourging, they extend the full length of the body, suggesting full nudity at both the time of flogging or flaying *and* during crucifixion. In the Pereire gem, which shows the cross from the front, the nudity is especially obvious and an erect penis can be discerned. In the Palatine graffito, the figure is depicted as wearing a donkey's head (or perhaps actually having a donkey's head) and as wearing a tunic to just above the buttocks. It would not be fully correct to say that he is naked, but he seems to be naked from the waist down, as evidenced by the visible curvature of the uncovered buttocks. His genitals would therefore be visible from the front view, even if this is not shown in the image.

A third significant point, which will be discussed later, with regard to crucifixion and impalement, is the trajectory of the upright. In the Puteoli graffito the main upright seems to undergo a marked narrowing halfway up where it comes into contact with the buttocks, and it then quickly widens out again. For the Pereire gem, the upright also seems to narrow and disappear into the body (or perhaps behind the body) at the crotch. The course of the upright after this is unclear, but it might be imagined to reappear from the victim's lower back unseen by the viewer and presumably join with the crossbeam behind the figure's head. For the Palatine graffito, it is very hard to discern the path of the upright with confidence, but it seems to disappears into the victim body between his buttocks and then re-emerges from the lower back.[23]

Unlike the later conventional images of crucifixion, these early depictions raise the disturbing possibility that the cross may have involved a penetrative sexual element in addition to the enforced nakedness clearly indicated in the gospel accounts. All three images include a crossbeam, indicating crucifixion, but they also each contain elements suggestive of both penetration from the upright and of sexualisation. Two of them, the Pereire gem and Palatine graffito, are intended as images of Jesus. They are earliest images of Jesus' crucifixion available. Images from Christian artists do not start to appear until two centuries later.

To assess the possibility of sexualised violence in crucifixion further, I will now turn to the historical development of crucifixion. Here, there are challenges that make drawing definitive conclusions surprisingly difficult.

From Assyrian Impalement to Roman Crucifixion

Scholarly accounts of Roman crucifixion often describe crucifixion as evolving from earlier impalement practices (Taylor 2008). It is common for accounts of the historical background to outline this progression through punitive innovations introduced by the Persians, which were learned by the Greeks (from Alexander the Great onwards), then adopted by the Carthaginians, and then developed by the Romans into what is now recognised as crucifixion.

Martin Hengel's book *Crucifixion* gives an overview of the historical development along these lines. One of Hengel's primary aims is to explain why crucifixion was viewed with such horror as an acutely shameful and degrading punishment, and he presents a vivid account of ancient sources. His book is justly called a classic, and the English translation was for many years the standard reference work on crucifixion. However, in recent years important new works have been published which go into much greater detail on the Greek and Roman sources.[24] These works add substantial detail to Hengel's work and also show that some of his interpretation must be viewed with a degree of circumspection. Caution is required over what the term 'crucifixion' means prior to the Roman period and how far the elements of crucifixion can be traced back into earlier periods. As the debate between Gunnar Samuelsson (2011) and John Granger Cook (2014) shows, the task of reconstructing what ancient writers mean by the Greek and Latin terms for cross and crucifixion prior to the first century—and in Samuelsson's view even in the first century—is far from straightforward.

The terminology for Roman crucifixion is more precise in Latin than in Greek, but even the Latin terms present difficulties. Some of the problems can be illustrated by a consideration of references to the cross and crucifixion in the gospels. Thus, the New Testament writers usually use variants of the Greek term *stauros* (which in other contexts means 'stake' or 'pole') for the cross, and the related verb *stauroō*, 'to crucify'. An example of the difficulty of knowing exactly what they had in mind can be illustrated in the gospel accounts where Jesus (Matt. 27:32, Mark 15:21, and Luke 23:26)—or Simon (John 19:17)—is said to carry the 'cross' to Golgotha. Most commentators suggest that due to the weight involved it is more plausible that only the crossbeam would be carried. In Latin, the crossbeam is designated more precisely (*patibulum*), but the gospels are written in Greek and use *stauros*.[25] The gospel writers may have assumed that it would have been obvious to any reader familiar with Roman crucifixion that only the crossbeam was intended. However, translation of *stauros* into the Latin Vulgate gives the impression that it was the full two-piece cross, not just the crossbeam, because *crucem* (from *crux*) rather than *patibulum* is used. Carrying the two-piece cross has become the familiar depiction in most Christian art. The uncertainty over 'the cross' that was carried is just one example that illustrates the challenges in understanding the details of a Roman crucifixion, especially in sources like the New Testament that refer to a Roman practice in Greek and then become widely known through a Latin translation. It is often hard to know what was intended by *stauros* and related words in ancient sources. The current section seeks to explain why many references to 'crucifixion' are therefore hard to interpret with precision. The discussion is introductory but is intended to give enough detail to convey the complexity and some of the areas of uncertainty on what many Christians take for granted.

Hengel makes only brief mention of Assyrian impalement punishments in the eighth and seventh centuries BCE; his investigation of the emergence of crucifixion commences in the era of the Persian Empire, from the sixth century BCE. Given the importance of impalement for the consideration of crucifixion in the next section of this chapter, however, it is useful to summarise some of the historical background on impalement before turning to the Persian period.

Assyrian images in the British Museum from the eighth and seventh centuries BCE show impalement as a punishment for enemies and as a means for public display of military power during siege warfare (Radner 2015, 104). In many cases, victims were probably dead prior to impalement, and the display served further to humiliate victims and those associated with them. In warfare, the spectacle of impaled corpses could be a way to intimidate those within a besieged city. Nonetheless, in at least some cases, the Assyrians also used impalement to execute living victims. In 866 BCE, Assurnasirpal impaled living enemy captives to terrify and overawe a besieged city. An inscription on the walls of the Ninurta temple at Kalhu confirms this practice: 'I impaled on stakes live troops around his city' (Radner 2015, 105).

Images show that the Assyrians used both 'longitudinal' and 'transversal' impalement on single upright stakes. In longitudinal impalements, such as at the siege of Dagibu (857 BCE), the impaling stake penetrates the full length of the torso upwards and vertically. Images suggest that the stake entered between the legs and came to rest somewhere in the upper body. In some cases, the stake might have penetrated upwards through the upper body and come out at the shoulder or upper back. In longitudinal impalement, where the stake enters between the legs, the most likely point of entry was the rectum (Radner 2015, 104).[26] By contrast, in a transversal impalement, the stake entered the upper body through the abdomen or chest. The top end of the stake might then rest within the rib cage or it might continue through the body and emerge on the other side of the torso. The wider end of the tapered stake was then planted firmly in the ground, raising the victim into the air.[27] If the stake was sufficiently tapered from top to base, the victim could be held aloft on the stake in a longitudinal or transversal impalement without slipping down.

A bronze relief that once decorated the wooden gates of the Mamu temple at Balawat (near modern Mosul) shows a longitudinal impalement scene from the siege of Dagibu (during the reign of Shalmaneser III (858–824 BCE). Six men are shown on top of single poles that enter their bodies between their spread legs (Radner 2015, 123, fig. 1). Another panel from the same gate shows the capture of Kullimeri (852 BCE). Assyrian soldiers are shown chopping the hands and feet off victims and then longitudinally impaling the remaining torso (Radner 2015, 123, fig. 3). A later series of reliefs from Nineveh shows the conquest of Lachish, a town in the Kingdom of Northern Israel, which fell to the Assyrians in 701 BCE, during the reign of Assyrian King Sennacherib (704–681 BCE). Reference to the siege is made in 2 Kings 18, 2 Chronicles 32 and Micah 1:13, as well as the Assyrian records and depictions in palace reliefs now at the British Museum. These reliefs show transversal impalement (Radner 2015, 125, fig. 7).

In each case, only a few victims are shown, but it is likely that they are representative of a much greater number. In some cases the victims were flayed first and their beaten skin displayed (Radner 2015, 107). The longitudinally impaled men at Dagibu and Kullimeri, and the transversally impaled men at Lachish, are all shown naked. As discussed in Chapter 1, forced nudity is a form of sexualised violence in its own right. In addition to this, longitudinal impalement should also be seen as extreme sexualised violence, whether the victims were alive or not.

The Assyrian Empire fell to the Babylonians in 610 BCE, and in 539 BCE the Babylonian Empire fell to the Persians. It is at this point that Hengel starts his historical overview of crucifixion as a punishment. Hengel notes (1977, 22): 'As a rule, books on the subject say that crucifixion began among the Persians'. Herodotus of Halicarnassus, a Greek historian in the fifth century BCE, is usually cited in support of this. A number of passages in Herodotus indicate victims being affixed with nails to a stake or pole for a prolonged death. Herodotus uses the verb the verb *anastauroun* for some of these. Since the verb *stauroō* is used in the New Testament for crucifixion, it is likely that these Persian *anastauroun* punishments probably approximated in some way to early versions of crucifixion. However, because the terms 'cross' and 'crucify' have come to be loaded with assumptions shaped by the image of Roman crucifixions in traditional Christian art, such as the crossbeam, there is a danger of reading too much from later practice into these accounts of 'crucifixions' in the Persian period. When words related to *stauros* and *stauroō* appear in Herodotus, it is more cautious to understand the instrument of execution as 'pole' or 'stake'. If the word 'cross' is used, then it is important to recognise that it may be different from a Roman cross. Likewise, when the verb *anastauroun* is used it appears to describe some form of suspension punishment, but it usually leaves the nature of the suspension unclear.

To add to uncertainty, in some cases the victim might have been executed in a manner closer to impalement than crucifixion, pierced by a stake, rather than tied or nailed to it. Hengel concedes that the form of crucifixion varied considerably and that the distinction between impalement and crucifixion in ancient sources is not always clear. He also points out that it can be difficult to tell whether a victim was still alive before being placed on the stake or pole, or if a corpse is displayed after execution. He notes that both practices were intended to signal the 'utmost indignity' (1977, 24). He also notes that Herodotus typically uses the Greek verb *anaskolopizein* (the noun *skolops* means pole) when referring to living victims, whereas he uses *anastauroun* when speaking of a dead corpse.[28]

In the fourth century BCE, the Persian Empire fell to the Hellenised empire led by Macedonian Alexander the Great. Hengel traces 'crucifixions' in the sources for this period as well, but these, too, invariably raise questions. For example, following the siege of Tyre (322 BCE), Alexander is reported to have executed 2,000 men. In the account by Diodorus Siculus the word *kremannumi* is used, which usually means 'hung up' (*The Library of History*, 17.46.4). Hengel (1977, 73), and the Loeb translation of Diodorus, and others, take this to be a form of crucifixion: 'The king sold the women and children into slavery and crucified all the men of military age'. But how close these 'crucifixions' were to Roman crucifixions is hard to determine.[29]

Similar questions might be asked about references to Carthaginian 'crucifixions' during the Punic Wars in the third century BCE.[30] Livy says the Carthaginians used crucifixion against their own generals as a punishment for failure in war (*History of Rome*, 38.48.13). Since Livy is writing in Latin, and using the terminology of *crux*, it is more likely that the executions he records would approximate to Roman crucifixion, but how closely even Carthaginian crucifixions correspond with Roman crucifixions is still an open question.

To sum up, if Hengel is correct, some sort of suspension punishment (as distinct from earlier impalements) was used by the Persians to create a slower and more protracted punishment. References to these punishments can be traced forward through the Greeks and the Carthaginians, and the term 'crucifixion' is often applied but should be viewed with some caution. These pre-Roman 'crucifixions' probably provided the stepping stones from the use of impalement by the Assyrians to the distinctive form of crucifixion used by the Romans.[31]

One notable feature of the scholarship is that most contributors agree that crucifixion was different from impalement, due to the way by which the victim was affixed to the cross and the protracted death that ensued from this. There also seems to be the assumption that because the Romans used crucifixion, they made no use of impalement. A consequence of separating crucifixion from impalement in this way, and viewing crucifixion as a replacement for impalement, is that the disturbing questions that might be raised about impalement—as a form of sexualised violence—have generally not been asked in relation to Roman crucifixions.

Crucifixion 57

At least in New Testament studies, this assumption appears to be seen as so self-evident that it does not even need to be acknowledged, never mind justified. Perhaps this is because the Romans are viewed as a 'civilised' society which modern democratic societies historically identify with in different ways. This discourages close concern for the cruelty and intentional indignity of Roman crucifixion and offers little support for investigation of crucifixion as penetrative sexualised violence. However, in the next section, I wish to argue that the relationship between impalement and crucifixion requires more consideration. Three passages in Seneca the Younger indicate that the Romans practised some form of impalement. These passages indicate that Roman use of impalement either occurred alongside crucifixion or as part of crucifixion. To this end, I will first review the evidence in Seneca and what it suggests for Roman crucifixion practice in general. Then I will explore a passage from Justin Martyr, which appears to suggest some form of impalement played a part in the crucifixion of Jesus.

Roman Impalement?

In 'Letter to Marcia on Consolation' (c. 40–45 CE) and *Moral Letters to Lucilius* (64 CE), the first-century Roman philosopher Seneca the Younger provides three separate passages that suggest elements of impalement in Roman crucifixion.

First, in his 'Letter to Marcia on Consolation' in *Moral Essays*, Seneca records a scene he witnessed during the campaign in Bithynia:

> I see crosses [*cruces*] there, not just of one kind but made in many different ways: some have their victims with head down to the ground; some impale their private parts; others stretch out their arms on the gibbet.
> (*Moral Essays*, 6.20.3)

Here Seneca refers to crosses (*cruces* from the root *crux*) of different kinds. He reports that at least some *cruces* are constructed so that the *stipitem* (from *stipes*, meaning the upright stake or stick) 'impale the private parts' (*per obscena stipitem egerunt*).

A second reference to crosses and to impalement using similar language appears in the letter titled 'Withdrawing from the World' in the *Moral Letters to Lucilius*, which is a collection of 124 letters.[32] This says:

> Picture to yourself under this head the prison, the cross [*cruces*], the rack, the hook, and the stake [*stipitem*] which they drive straight through a man until it protrudes from his throat'.
> (*Epistles*, 14.5)

In the second passage, the cross is listed alongside other punishments. These punishments include what seems to be impalement, which in this case is said to go '*per medium hominem qui per os emergeret stipitem*'. This is translated above as 'the stake which they drive straight through a man until it protrudes from his throat'. This suggests the upright (*stipitem*) goes through the middle of the body (*per medium*), which implies longitudinal impalement. In both passages the Latin word used for the actual instrument of impalement is *stipitem* (upright or stick) rather than the word *crux*. In the 'Letter to Marcia', the *stipitem* appears to be an integral part of the *crux*, whereas in 'Withdrawing from the World' the *stipitem* seems to involve a different form of punishment that is to be distinguished from the *crux*.

A third passage, in a letter titled 'The Futility of Planning', which is also in *Moral Letters to Lucilius* (*Epistles*, 101), is much longer and in some ways more cryptic. It features Seneca's encouragement to Lucilius to live a noble and manly life. To illustrate his point, Seneca pours scorn on the pitiful and unmanly Maecenas (*Moral Letters*, 101.10–14). Seneca complains that Maecenas is so debased by his fear of death that he would cling to life rather than embrace a noble death. Seneca says Maecenas would even do this when all that he could possibly hope for in life would be the worst imaginable suffering and disgrace. Thus Maecenas would be willing to suffer weakness or deformity just to prolong the breath of life a little longer. To illustrate the absurdity of such dishonourable behaviour, Seneca pictures Maecenas as wanting his life to endure even if he were enduring crucifixion. He presents Maecenas as saying:

> Fashion me with a palsied hand, Weak of foot, and a cripple; Build upon me a crook-backed hump; Shake my teeth till they rattle; All is well, if my life remains. Save, oh, save it, I pray you, Though I sit on the piercing cross!
>
> (*Epistles*, 101.11)

Seneca despises this attitude, and argues instead that crucifixion is so awful and so unmanly that a 'real' Roman man would welcome death rather than prefer the misery and indignity of clinging to life on a cross:

> There he [Maecenas] is, praying for that which, if it had befallen him, would be the most pitiable thing in the world! And seeking a postponement of suffering, as if he were asking for life! I should deem him most despicable had he wished to live up to the very time of crucifixion: 'Nay,' he cries, 'you may weaken my body if you will only leave the breath of life in my battered and ineffective carcass! Maim me if you will, but allow me, misshapen and deformed as I may be, just a little more time in the world! You may nail me up and set my seat upon the piercing cross!'
>
> (*Epistles* 101.12)

Seneca firmly rejects this:

> Is it worth while to weigh down upon one's own wound, and hang impaled upon a gibbet, that one may but postpone something which is the balm of troubles, the end of punishment? Is it worth all this to possess the breath of life only to give it up?
>
> (*Epistles* 101.12)

Seneca's references to crucifixion in this passage are striking, in both what they say and what they imply.

On the one hand, Seneca does not give a sufficiently clear or detailed account of crucifixion to show someone not so familiar with crucifixion why the cross was seen as so horrific and demeaning. The degradation of the cross is either well known, or inappropriate to discuss, or both. On the other hand, Seneca mentions some significant and troubling details. The passage suggests, for instance, that in at least some cases Roman crucifixion cannot be clearly separated from impalement. Sitting on the piercing cross, is explicitly mentioned twice: 'Though I sit on the piercing cross' (*vel acuta Si sedeam cruce*, 101.11) and 'you may nail me up and set my seat upon the piercing cross!' (*et acutam sessuro crucem*, 101.12). It is then suggested a third time, when Seneca asks, 'Is it worthwhile to weigh down upon one's own wound, and hang impaled upon a gibbet?' (*et patibulo pendere districtum*, 101.12).

Seneca asks, 'What does he mean by such womanish and indecent verse' (*carminis effeminati turpitudo*, 101.13). The piercing involved in the 'piercing cross' might initially be interpreted as a reference to nails. However, the passage suggests Seneca has more in mind than nails piercing hands or feet. The linking of sitting and piercing in 'sit on the piercing cross' and 'set my seat on the piercing cross', and the use of the singular 'wound' (*vulnus*) in the phrase 'to weigh down upon one's wound', suggest that the piercing is associated with the sitting.

These three passages from Seneca are included in many discussions of Roman crucifixion, and the references to impalement are often mentioned in at least some way. However, the passages have not prompted a serious debate on the use of impalement in Roman crucifixions, including the crucifixion of Jesus. Cook, who offers a more detailed discussion than many scholars, notes that the passages in both the 'Letter to Marcia' and the 'Withdrawing from the World' refer to *crux* (in the nominative plural form, *cruces*), but Seneca uses the term *stipes* (in the singular accusative form, *stipitem*) for the impalements rather than the term *crux*. Although this is true, Cook's claim that the *stipes* should be seen as separate from the *crux* is less compelling. Separating *stipes* and *crux* is persuasive for reading the passage from 'Withdrawing from the World', where it looks like two distinct punishments are being described, but this does not work so well for the passages in 'Letter to Marcia' or for 'The Futility of Planning'. In 'Letter to Marcia', the *stipes* which impales is part of the *crux* and not separate from it. Likewise, in 'The Futility of Planning', it is the *crux* itself—or some part of it—that is described as 'piercing'.

What Seneca has in mind in 'The Futility of Planning' is not completely clear. However, the most natural reading is what has been translated as 'I sit on the piercing cross', 'weigh down upon one's wound', and 'hang impaled' is evidence of some form of impalement incorporated into crucifixion. How such incorporation was achieved is not explained. One possibility is that a victim might have been impaled in a way similar to the longitudinal Assyrian impalement. Read in this way, the main upright (*stipes*) of the cross might be understood as penetrating the body, and this seems to be in line with the 'Withdrawing from the World' passage where 'they drive straight through a man until it protrudes from his throat' (*Epistles*, 14.5).[33]

A different way to imagine what Seneca has in mind in 'The Futility of Planning' is a structure involving a more traditional two-piece cross, especially because this passage mentions a crossbeam (*patibulum*). One possibility for such a cross is illustrated in a book by Robert Knox from the seventeenth century. Knox was held captive in Ceylon (present-day Sri Lanka) and subsequently wrote of his experiences and observations. His account (Knox 1681, 40) includes a description of punishments he says were used by the king:

> At the place of Execution, there are always some [bodies] sticking upon Poles, others hanging up in quarters upon Trees. . . . This place is always in the greatest High-way, that all may see and stand in awe. For which end this is his constant practice.

The illustration titled 'One Impaled on a Stake' that accompanies the passage shows how a two-piece cross with a narrow upright could longitudinally impale a victim (Knox 1681, 38).[34]

Although longitudinal impalement on a two-piece cross in the manner depicted by Knox would have feasible in Roman times, it is not clear that an execution of this sort would have been deemed a crucifixion. Both Samuelsson and Cook agree that crucifixion involved a protracted death, and they reject longitudinal impalement for this reason. However, the Romans might have introduced innovations to crucifixion to both intensify and prolong punishment. As noted earlier, Josephus (*Jewish War* 5.446–452) records experimentation and innovation during the siege of Jerusalem. It is possible that the Romans devised a cross which could impale a victim *and* facilitate a slow death.

A *sedile* (seat or peg) on the upright might achieve more suffering and humiliation and a slower death. As noted earlier, a *sedile* would normally give the victim additional support. By taking some of the victim's body weight, a *sedile* would reduce the burden on the chest and pressure on the lungs, and thereby prolong the death process. A short sharp *sedile* attached to the upright at an angle to make a horn could impale a victim. This would allow for the slow death associated with crucifixion whilst also enacting the perceived disgrace of sexualised violation. In fact, this might function in much the same way as the non-fatal use of 'the stick' in Libya. If a crucifixion victim was seated on the peg, and their hands or wrists attached to the crossbeam, the cross would inflict a drawn-out and particularly ignominious death. A form of self-impalement on the *sedile* is therefore one plausible reading of Seneca's words 'I set my seat on the piercing cross'.

The position of the victim in the Pereire gem might suggest that the artist assumed the crucifixion of Jesus to involve something along these lines, though as noted above there may be some tension between this image and the implication in John 19:31–33 that Jesus' legs were supporting his body.

In 'Crucifixion, State Terror, and Sexual Abuse', I note the impalement reference in Seneca's 'Letter to Marcia' (*Moral Essays*, 6.20.3), but at the time it seemed to me to be an outlier (Tombs 1999, 101). However, the additional references in 'Withdrawing from the World' (*Epistles*, 14.5) and 'The Futility of

Planning' (*Epistles* 101.10–14) require reconsideration of this. They strengthen the possibility that the Romans used impalement alongside crucifixion and in some cases as part of crucifixion.

This is not to say that all and every Roman cross involved impalement or that this is evidence for what happened in the case of Jesus. There are tensions and difficulties in the evidence. 'Withdrawing from the World' suggests that impalement was used alongside crucifixion but implies that they were two different punishments. If this were our sole evidence, it would not be hard to integrate this passage with the conventional understanding of Roman crucifixions. We could conclude that impalement and crucifixion were simply two different and discrete punishments and that the Romans sometimes used both impalement and crucifixions. However, 'Letter to Marcia' and 'The Futility of Planning' both suggest that impalement was used *in crucifixion*, although neither gives sufficient detail to explain *how* this happened.

Further research by biblical scholars and classicists is required to assess how these passages in Seneca are to be understood and what difference they make to the understanding of Roman crucifixion. However, before concluding, there is one further piece of evidence on Jesus' crucifixion, offered by Justin Martyr, that should be noted.

Justin was a second-century Christian apologist born in Samaria. He speaks of Jesus as the Paschal lamb in his *Dialogue with Trypho* (c. 160 CE). More specifically, a passage in the dialogue makes a startling connection between Jesus on the cross and the spitting or skewering of the lamb:

> For the lamb, which is roasted, is roasted and dressed up in the form of the cross. For one spit is transfixed right through from the lower parts up to the head, and one across the back, to which are attached the legs of lamb.
> (Justin, *Dialogue with Trypho*, 40)[35]

Here Justin compares the form of the cross to the spitting of the lamb, with one spit running the length of the lamb and a second spit spreading the lamb's legs. The connection that Justin draws between Jesus and the Paschal lamb (in terms of the lamb's being transfixed from the lower parts upwards) may reflect his assumption of some form of impalement in Jesus' crucifixion.

Given the timing of Jesus' death in relation to Passover, and the faith that developed in the Christian community, which saw the cross as sacrificial and salvific, the identification of Jesus as Paschal lamb originates well before Justin's writing and can be found as early as 1 Corinthians 5.7. However, Justin's words suggest that this identification might offer a hidden clue into the nature of crucifixion. The passage suggests that the idea of impalement at the cross was not unthinkable for an influential second-century Christian. It is also notable that Justin did not feel the need to explain to his audience in any detail how the spitting of the Paschal lamb could be similar to Jesus' crucifixion. It is unlikely that Justin would make this suggestion about Jesus' experience unless he believed it to be true. It must be said that just because Justin believed something to be true does not in itself provide proof that it happened this way. It does, however, provide a viewpoint from early Christian writings. This view supports the concern that the impalement accounts of crucifixion preserved in Seneca may be relevant to understanding the crucifixion of Jesus.

Conclusion

This chapter has considered whether some form of impalement might have played a role within Roman crucifixions. It has raised questions over possible overlaps between crucifixion and impalement, and whether the relationship between impalement and crucifixion in the first century is best understood as an either/or alternative, or whether in some cases impalement and crucifixion might have been a cruel both/and combination.

Seneca's observations suggest that crucifixion was at least sometimes combined with impalement, and we cannot know if these cases were rare exceptions or part of more common practice. Josephus might offer further support for this, but is more suggestive than explicit (*Jewish War*, 5.541). The Pereire gem and the Palatine graffito are the earliest available pictorial images of Jesus' crucifixion and they both might be viewed as suggesting sexual violence but are hard to interpret with confidence. Justin's reference is striking but cryptic.

While we may know more about the practices of the time from this discussion, we do not know what happened to Jesus. The most reasonable conclusion from all this is that the possibility of Jesus' brutal and sexualised humiliation on the cross cannot be ruled out and deserves further consideration and research. It appears that subjecting a political prisoner to brutal and sexualised humiliation on the cross would not have been inconsistent with the practices of the time.

Notes

1 Josephus (*Life of Flavius Josephus*, 75) describes a crucifixion during which he recognised three of his former acquaintances and asked Titus to release them. One survived, but the other two died.
2 Trypho may be a fictional character but the view of the cross he offers suggests how crucifixion was seen. See also Justin, *Dialogue*, 32.1 and 89.2.
3 The census revolt of 6 CE, when Quirinius was Governor of Syria (6–7 CE) and Coponius Procurator of Judea (6–9 CE), also met with widespread reprisals; Josephus, *Jewish War* 2.117–118; *Ant*. 18.1–10.
4 In a similar way, in Judges 19, the events leading up to the rape and torture of the Levite's wife are told in great detail, but the rape and torture itself is simply stated with minimal further detail, beyond it lasting 'all through the night' (Judg. 19:25).
5 On earlier symbolic representation of crucifixion from the third century, see Hurtado (2013). Symbols included the staurograms (combining the Greek letters *tau* and *rho*) and the Christogram (combining the letters *chi* and *rho*).
6 For 'Crucifixion' by Rembrandt (1631): https://en.wikipedia.org/wiki/Christ_on_the_Cross_%28Rembrandt%29.
7 A third form of *crux compacta* was the *crux decussata*, with two diagonal beams attached together (X), but this variant will be given less attention in what follows. The designation of the *crux simplex* as a cross might seem strange, because in English the

idea of a cross typically suggests two elements which 'cross' each other, as in the *cross descutta* (X). However, the Latin word *crux* does not carry the same implication.
8   It says: 'because the cross in the T was to have grace' (*Epistle of Barnabas*, 9.7; Lightfoot 1907, 278). Lucian of Samosata says that the letter 'T' was seen as an evil letter because of the evil form of execution that was shaped in the form of an upper case *tau*; see Hengel (1977, 8).
9   For an example of a Tau cross, see 'Crucifixion' by Konrad Witz (c 1444): https://en.wikipedia.org/wiki/Tau_cross#/media/File:Konrad_Witz_005.jpg.
10 There has been discussion over whether or not nails through the hands could have supported the weight of the body without the hands tearing unless there was provision of further support from ropes or cords. Christian art has often shown the nails (or the wounds) in the middle of the palm, but it has long been known that most of the palm would be too flimsy to support the full weight of the body; Pierre Barbet, *A Doctor at Calvary: The Passion of Our Lord Jesus Christ as Described by a Surgeon* (New York: Doubleday, 1953). For this reason, it is more likely that nailing was through the wrist bones. However, Zugibe has argued that there may be at least one further location on the upper palm (close to the wrist) which might have been strong enough; see Zugibe (1989).
11 For Jesus, Pilate had written 'Jesus of Nazareth, the King of the Jews' in Aramaic, Latin, and Greek (John 19:19–22); see also Matt. 27:37, Mark 15:26, and Luke 23:38. In art this often appears as abbreviated Latin using the letters 'INRI'.
12 See, for example, 'Christ Crucified', by Diego Velázquez (1632): https://commons.wikimedia.org/wiki/File:Diego_Velázquez_007.jpg.
13 John has some other details which are different to the Synoptics, including the time of crucifixion and its date in relation to Passover. John also includes the piercing of Jesus' side with a spear (John 19:34), and this wound is often shown in art. On the sexualised representation of Jesus' side wound as a vulva in medieval art, see Easton (2006). See also Steinberg (1983) and Trexler (1993).
14 Hermann Fulda (1878) argues that Jesus was probably executed with his hands secured above his head on a single upright stake (*crux simplex*). Jehovah's Witnesses follow the tradition that Jesus was crucified with his hands secured about his head on a *crux simplex* without a crossbeam: www.jw.org/en/bible-teachings/questions/did-jesus-die-on-cross/.
15 In John 20:25, Thomas asks to put his finger in the mark left by the nails in Jesus' hands. This is taken as evidence that Jesus' hands were punctured with nails, and he is widely pictured with bleeding wounds in his palms. Thomas does not mention the mark of the nails in Jesus' feet, so it is not clear from the text whether or not Jesus' feet were nailed to the upright. However, Psalm 21:16 refers to piercing both hands and feet, and Justin Martyr writes: 'Through another prophet, he says, "They pierced my hands and my feet, and for my vesture they cast lots"' (*Apology*, 35).
16 Tzaferis 1985, 52.
17 A skeleton with a nail through the back of the right foot has recently been discovered in Britain, in a third-century cemetery in the Cambridgeshire village of Fenstanton (Key 2021). It is believed that this provides a second archaeological example of crucifixion.
18 See also Horace's reference to slaves 'feeding crows on the cross', *Epist.* 1.16.46–48, cited in O'Collins (1992, 1208). These further indignities on the body, and Jewish belief that people are created in the image of God and the human form should be respected, may help to explain why Deuteronomy 21:22–23 views hanging as a particular curse and the consequent avoidance of leaving bodies to hang after death. Reports on abuses committed by security forces in El Salvador and Guatemala during the 1980s suggest that the areas of a victim's body that carrion birds were most likely to attack first were the soft areas of the face (especially the eyes and the lips) and the genital region. If the victim was placed close enough to the ground, the body could be exposed to other beasts as well. See especially Josephus, *Jewish War* 4.310.

19 Cook includes a photo and a helpful outline drawing by Antonio Lombatti (Cook 2014, 456–457). Images of the drawing are also available online: for example, www.roger-pearse.com/weblog/2017/01/13/the-crucifixion-graffito-of-alkimilla-from-puteoli/.
20 The Greek inscription '*Alkimila*' is written above the graffito. This is more probably a feminine name, so if the figure is indeed male, *Alkimila* is probably not the name of the figure in the depiction. It either refers to someone else or it might be used to suggest that the male figure is being feminised through crucifixion.
21 A photo is included in Cook (2014, 459), and a line drawing that was first published by Raffaele Garrucci (1856) is in Harley-McGowan (2019b, 110); images are also available at https://en.wikipedia.org/wiki/Alexamenos_graffito.
22 Tacitus writes that Nero blamed a fire in Rome on Christians and punished them in cruel ways (64 CE): 'They were covered with wild beasts' skins and torn to death by dogs; or they were fastened on crosses, and, when daylight failed were burned to serve as lamps by night' (*Annals*, 15.44). It is possible that the artist had heard of the Christians being punished in animal skins and conflated the details in the mockery of the graffito. In another disturbing detail, Suetonius reports that Nero also sometimes had a game in which he himself wore an animal skin and attacked victims who were bound to stakes (*stipitem*): 'Covered with the skin of some wild animal, he [Nero] was let loose from a cage and attacked the private parts of men and women, who were bound to stakes' (Suetonius, *Lives of the Caesars*, 6.29).
23 The line drawing by Raffaele Garrucci shows the upright in a continuous line behind the victim, but the photo suggests otherwise.
24 These include Chapman (2008), Samuelsson (2011), Cook (2014), and Chapman and Schnabel (2015). Each of these excellent works offers richly detailed argumentation and the convenience of well-presented extracts from the primary sources.
25 In a similar way, see Chariton, *Callirhoe*, 4.2.7: 'They were duly brought out, chained together at foot and neck, each carrying his own cross. The executioners added this grim public spectacle to the requisite penalty as a deterrent to others so minded'. In this passage, the Greek word *stauron* is used for 'cross'.
26 Anal impalement could be facilitated by widening the entry point with a knife. For one version of the brutal steps in longitudinal impalement, see the account by Ivo Andrić, *The Bridge on the Drina*, trans. Lovett F. Edwards (London: George Allen and Unwin, 1959 [orig. 1945]). For impaled women, vaginal entry was also possible.
27 When displaying a dead victim, the stake in a transversal impalement need not in every case penetrate the body. Radner suggests that for the display of corpses, some stakes or poles might have had an additional crossbeam piece at the top to make a T-shaped end. This could then be used to lift and support the dead victim's body with the corpse slumped over the top and held up but not penetrated. It is unlikely that this would have been sufficiently secure to keep a live victim in place, but the designation of this form of elevated display as 'impalement' suggests the wider range of meanings the term covered during the Assyrian period.
28 Herodotus, *Hist*. 1:128.2; 3:125.3; 3:132.2; 3:159.1. After Herodotus, the verbs appear to be used synonymously in Greek sources. O'Collins (1992, 1207) notes that Josephus uses only (*ana*)*stauroun*, whereas Philo uses only *anaskolopizein*. Thus whilst the use of *anastauroun* by Herodotus might suggest proximity with what is understood as crucifixion in the New Testament, the use of the term in Herodotus seems to be different from its use in the gospel narratives. Herodotus uses it for post-mortem display and humiliation, not execution. Conversely, the gospels never use *skolops* for the cross, and although Herodotus uses it for live victims, *anaskolopizein*, these passages in his work could be readily translated as impalement rather than crucifixion. Recent scholarship has suggested that a useful distinction to tell accounts of impalement and crucifixion apart is that impalement is associated with a quick death (Samuelsson 2011, 29; Cook 2014, 2). When descriptions of Persian executions suggest a more protracted death,

these passages therefore suggest a punishment other than impalement. In some cases, this distinction can shed light on whether a source had impalement or crucifixion in mind, but this is not always possible, especially if the death process in an execution is not described.

29 Cook argues that 'since Diodorus is a Roman author he probably envisioned these executions as crucifixions' (Cook 2014, 233). In support of this, Cook points out that Quintus Curtius Rufus also refers to this incident, and uses the Latin phrase *crucibus affixi* (*History of Alexander*, 4.4.17).

30 Hengel (1977, 23). On crucifixions during the Punic Wars see, for example, Livy, *History of Rome*, 22.13.9; 28.37.2; 38.48.13; Polybius, *The Histories*, 1.11.5; 1.24.6; 1.79.4–5; 1.86.4; and Diodorus Siculus, *The Library of History*, 25.5.2; 25.10.2; 26.23.1.

31 Recent works by Chapman (2008), Samuelsson (2011), Cook (2014), and Chapman and Schnabel (2015) show that the range of meaning for the Greek term *stauros* and Latin word *crux* can lead to divergent views on how much can be known with confidence on Persian, Greek, and Carthaginian 'crucifixions', and even when these terms are used for Roman crucifixions there is room for interpretation.

32 In the Loeb series, 'Withdrawing from the World' appears as *Epistle*, 14, and the Loeb translation and referencing are used here.

33 Justus Lipsius provides a line drawing of a *crux simplex infixionem* that impales in this way, and he references the three passages in Seneca (*Lipsi* 1606, 20): https://en.wikipedia.org/wiki/Impalement#/media/File:Empalement.jpg.

34 The illustration is available at www.gutenberg.org/files/14346/14346-h/14346-h.htm.

35 In Roberts and Donaldson (1885–96).

4 Resurrection

'And they shall name him Emmanuel', which means, 'God is with us'.

(Matthew 1.23)

For I am convinced that neither death, nor life, nor angels, nor rulers, nor things present, nor things to come, nor powers, nor height, nor depth, nor anything else in all creation, will be able to separate us from the love of God in Christ Jesus our Lord.

(Rom. 8.38–39)

Introduction

On Palm Sunday 2022, the Brazilian newspaper *Folha de Sao Paulo* published a feature article by the journalist Márvio dos Anjos in its colour supplement (Anjos 2022). The article discussed Jesus as a victim of sexual abuse. Anjos had approached me some months earlier when he read an article by Rosie Dawson published in the *Church Times* in the previous year (Dawson 2021b).

As we talked via Zoom calls between Brazil and New Zealand, dos Anjos told me he was initially sceptical, suspecting that it was a misguided and anachronistic attempt to make Jesus relevant to modern times. However, he knew about torture and abuses against political prisoners during the military regime (1964–85). In that context, he told me, he came to see how this reading of crucifixion could offer an important and timely message to the church. In his Palm Sunday article he set out to explain to a wider readership both why the claim is made and why it matters.

Anjos took great pains to avoid sensationalism and develop the argument carefully. Nonetheless, the reactions on Brazilian Twitter showed very different responses. Some were dismissive, even hostile. André Porciuncula (2022), a candidate for election as Federal Deputy (the Brazilian equivalent to Congress), tweeted: 'Easter is approaching and *Folha de São Paulo*, as a criminal organization, promotes this filthy attack against the Christian faith. I'll file a criminal complaint'. First Lady Michelle Bolsonaro (2022) tweeted:

> Insanity, Christophobia and lack of scruples. Do not be deceived: God is not mocked. For whatever a man sows, that he will also reap. GALATIANS 6.

More positive respondents on Twitter pointed out that these tweets sound like their authors have not read beyond the headline and that there is more to the issue. Some noted that the denunciations demonstrated the truth of one of the points in the article: those who claim to love Jesus are sometimes not interested in what happened to him. Moreover, in their outrage by any suggestion that he was a victim of sexual abuse, they did not seem to pause to reflect on the implications of their response.

Since my initial article on crucifixion in 1999, I have had the opportunity to collaborate with colleagues around the world who are working to address issues of abuse within churches and other communities. Some of these ideas have been shared in thoughtful Bible study groups, panel discussions and lectures, and also through print media like the Palm Sunday supplement. I have learned that the responses that greet the work can also show why it matters, and how it might lead from a focus on death, to an affirmation of life.

Following the way of the cross unavoidably involves confrontation with abusive and degrading practices: stripping, mocking, crucifixion. At one level, it is understandable that those who express a love for Jesus are shocked to read he experienced sexualised violence in any form.

Yet, at the same time, the outraged condemnation that meets an attempt to raise these questions reveals troubling assumptions about how they see those who have been subjected to and harmed by sexual violence. It is as if acknowledging sexual abuse would mean seeing Jesus as damaged or lessened. This in turn, means he could no longer, it seems, be loved, or perhaps respected, in the same way as a saviour figure. This attitude may be linked to an unexamined attitude that sees survivors of abuse in our time as irreparably diminished.

Few Christians would admit to blaming victims of sexual abuse or express negative views of survivors openly or explicitly. However, some responses to the presentation of Jesus as a victim of abuse bring such attitudes to the surface, sometimes forcefully. The purpose of this work is not to shock or provoke, or to diminish Christianity or Christians. However, when the work is criticised as provocative and shocking, this can offer a valuable opportunity for new thinking.

This opportunity does not often arise in the context of social media. But in a thoughtful and appropriate pastoral context, it can offer an important teaching moment within churches. Strong feelings and hidden judgements can offer the church a chance to open up an honest conversation about underlying attitudes that are deeply held and harmful.

The assumptions and myths behind these negative responses need to be carefully interrogated. Recognising that stripping and enforced nudity were used in intentional ways to mock Jesus, and identifying this as an issue of concern for the church, is not the same as 'mocking Jesus' or as 'Christophobia'. On the contrary, it should be a way of taking seriously the suffering of Jesus.

Jesus' experience is both a challenge and an invitation. It invites churches to develop a more serious theological conversation on sexual violence and upholding human dignity. This conversation could help towards developing a better practical response to survivors.

There is no question that better survivor care is urgently needed. The fact of widespread abuse in religious settings—and by religious authorities—is indisputable. The #MeToo movement has exposed how prevalent sexual harassment and sexual assault is in wider society, and why need for churches to make a better response to this (Stiebert 2019). But how can survivors be supported if, by implication, the abuse they suffered and endured is seen as making them less worthy of love and respect? If Jesus is seen as worth less—or worthless—this suggests a similar attitude to other survivors.

This chapter explores how acknowledgement of the sexual violence against Jesus in crucifixion might offer opportunities for hope and healing, with particular attention to the recovery and reaffirmation of human dignity. To explore these opportunities, it is helpful to distinguish between the biblical, the theological, and the pastoral issues that are raised by the work. The biblical questions require careful attention to what the text does and doesn't say and how attention to past and present contexts can help towards a better understanding of both the violence and the silence. These biblical issues have been the main focus of Chapters 1, 2 and 3.

Many of the theological issues that arise deserve a book of their own. Among many other theological questions, the preceding chapters encourage renewed attention to what it means that Christ has shared the experience of human beings and was both fully human and fully divine. This in turn invites attention to theological reflection on the nature of God, the meaning of Emmanuel as 'God is with us' (Matt. 1:23), and the resurrection of Christ.

Above all, there are pastoral implications for working in church communities: how do we treat each other with dignity, and how can the church better respond to victims and survivors of sexual violence? This chapter shares some reflections on why this work is worth doing and what a sensitive and constructive pastoral contribution might look like. Embracing this conversation can help the church to improve its responses to those who experience sexual violence now, as shown in the liturgy for survivors of sexual abuse offered by Karen O'Donnell (2021, 271–273). Jesus' experience can be a challenge, and an invitation, to churches to reaffirm life-giving messages to survivors of sexual violence. Two of the most important of these messages are 'you are not alone' and 'you are not to blame'.

To be clear, nothing will ever make the sexualised violence against Jesus—or against anybody—something positive, or good, or worthwhile, or for the best. The positive message of Christian faith is to be found in Jesus' life, ministry, and resurrection, not in his suffering and crucifixion. However, his experience of crucifixion cannot be dismissed as a mere side issue. Jesus' life, ministry, and resurrection can only be fully grasped when understood in the shadow of his suffering and the cross. Recognising that Jesus was raised not just from death but from 'death on a cross' (Phil. 2:8) is a first step to seeing both the cross and resurrection for what they are. It is the first step to understanding why the relationship between the two elements—crucifixion and resurrection—is so important. Crucifixion was not just any death: death on the cross involved public terror, shame, disgrace, and scandal.

Blame and Stigma

In the book *The Second Assault*, Joyce Williams and Karen Holmes describe how women who experience sexual abuse are often subjected to a further, second assault of negative judgement from others. They write (Williams and Holmes 1981, xi):

> For women who are raped, the essence of the second assault is skepticism, blame, and even condemnation, emanating from society at large, from one's own community, from one's own self-blame (an internalization of the attitudes of others), from family, and from significant others.

Many victims and survivors experience the victim-blaming that Williams and Holmes describe. Their book draws on their work with women in the United States in the mid-1970s. However, the dynamics of secondary assault that they identify are applicable for understanding the impact of sexual violence more widely. Furthermore, as Williams and Holmes point out, the pattern is so well established that even survivors often blame themselves. The negative judgements of wider society are so relentless, and so readily absorbed by survivors, that survivors often carry a sense of self-blame regardless of whether or not they speak of their experiences. This 'second assault' is also known as 'secondary victimisation' or 'secondary harm' or even 'second rape' (Williams 1984; Madigan and Gamble 1989). Williams and Holmes, and many others, have described it as just as devastating as the first assault. They describe the second assault as 'perhaps more cruel in its compounding effect than the first' (Williams and Holmes 1981, xi).

To understand the long-term impact of the second assault, it is helpful to understand stigma and the ways that stigma interacts with blame and self-blame. Stigma is described by Erving Goffman as a 'spoiled identity' (Goffman 1963). Attention to the ways that stigma operates offers insight into the subtlety and complexity of victim-blaming. Attention to stigma shifts the question from 'who was responsible?' (which is the issue in blame) to 'who is seen as diminished?', regardless of whether or not they are to blame. For sexual violence, it is almost always the victim who is seen as diminished and who carries a heavy stigma, even when they are not directly blamed.

Looking at stigma in addition to blame is important because stigma is often more hidden. In the decades since Williams and Holmes published their research in 1981, many of the myths that support the direct blame elements in victim-blaming have been exposed, discussed, and publicly challenged and detoxified. There is now much greater public awareness on the mechanics of victim-blaming and the myths that wrongly sustain it. However, stigma often persists at a less obvious and less conscious level than direct blame, and it deserves attention in its own right.

The South African researcher Elisabet Le Roux (2014) addresses sexual violence, and the responses of the church, in different settings in the Global South. In a chapter that draws on a decade of work in many different countries, Le Roux (2021) discusses stories of women who experienced sexual violence. In many cases, the women interviewed feared that if their husbands discovered what had happened, they would be divorced and abandoned. In Colombia, they described the stigma they carried and feared that even their mothers might reject them.

In research commissioned by the Christian agency Tearfund, Le Roux found that many survivors look to the church as the institution that is best placed to support them in the aftermath of sexual violence (Tearfund 2011, 10). However, she shows that instead of offering active support and care, in many cases church leaders remain silent (Tearfund 2011, 8). Sexual violence was treated as shameful and taboo within the church, too. This silence reinforced the sense of shame and stigma experienced by survivors. Instead of feeling supported, survivors sensed an unspoken negative judgement against them in faith communities.

Alongside the silence, some survivors also experienced more direct criticism and discrimination. They shared stories of the harsh treatment they experienced at the hands of church leaders and members. As Le Roux reports, 'often the stigma and discrimination they experience from fellow church members and religious leaders are the most hurtful' (Le Roux 2021, 182). She shows how deep the prejudice against survivors can go within the churches by citing a male church member she interviewed in Sake, in the Democratic Republic of the Congo:

> For me, I do not think I can consider a woman who has been sexually violated. For me, she is no longer a perfect woman, because she has now been violated, she just lost her value. From my point of view I can no longer even go to her family, to look for a wife, because I know that family is already cursed, she is no longer valuable once sexually violated.
>
> (Le Roux 2021, 178)

Le Roux explains: 'These words . . . are a typical example of the stigma and discrimination that survivors of sexual violence face' (Le Roux 2021, 178). Survivors often report that the way others in the community respond to them harms them more than the original physical and sexual victimisation. Secondary victimisation is often longer-lasting, and involves more people, than the original violence. In addition, Le Roux points out that many survivors also self-stigmatise and internalise these harsh judgements. Survivors are therefore subjected to stigma within both the community and in the church, and they often carry self-stigma within themselves, even if they know that they are not to blame.

Based on her work with faith communities, Le Roux recognises the importance of initiatives by churches and Christian-based NGOs to address sexual violence (Le Roux et al. 2020). Sometimes faith leaders dismiss concern about sexual violence, saying it is outside of the core work of the church and/or a response to an external agenda (Tearfund 2011, 8). Le Roux argues that concern and compassion for others are Christian values; attention to biblical texts that the churches identify as authoritative can support and reinforce these values. Le Roux identifies the Contextual Bible Study (CBS) on crucifixion developed at the Ujamma Centre at the University of KwaZulu-Natal in Pietermaritzburg, South Africa, as a particularly helpful resource for this work (Le Roux 2021, 185).

CBS provides open-ended questions that guide participants through a 'slow reading' of the text, alongside attentiveness to details that are otherwise easily missed. It allows participants to offer their own thoughts, hear from each other, and explore textual issues in a dialogical way. This type of approach has the advantage that participants have more control over their own learning through a facilitated engagement with the text. This is a much deeper approach to learning than simple instruction. The CBS structures a discussion of Matthew 27:26–31 in a way that encourages everyone in the group to offer their thoughts and reflect on the challenges raised (Ujamaa Centre 2019).[1]

A Bible Study on the Crucifixion of Jesus

1. Listen to a 'slow' reading of Matthew 27:26–31 in a number of different translations and languages. What have you heard from this slow reading of a well-known story that disturbs you?
2. Who are the characters in this story, and what do we know about each of them?
3. What forms of violence are used against Jesus?
4. How many times is Jesus stripped? Matthew makes it clear that Jesus was stripped more than once. Re-read the text carefully and identify how many times Jesus is stripped.
5. Is stripping a form of violence? Why do the soldiers strip Jesus?
6. Matthew also makes it clear that Jesus was stripped in front of a whole 'cohort' of about 500 soldiers. What other forms of sexual abuse might have taken place when so many men were involved in the repeated stripping and beating of Jesus?
7. In what situations in your context are men sexually abused by other men?
8. Are there resources in your community to address male sexual violence against men?
9. What can we do to address the issue of male sexual violence against men? Devise a specific 'action plan' that you can participate in.

Exploring Jesus' experience of sexual violence through studies like this is valuable for faith communities in different ways. For example, discussion of Jesus' experience can prompt churches to interrogate examples of confused thinking about survivors. The belief that survivors are lessened or damaged in some way presents more obvious contradictions when applied to Jesus. Those who see Jesus as less of a saviour because he was subjected to abuse struggle to explain their reasoning in ways that withstand scrutiny. On reflection, most recognise that Jesus should not be seen as defiled or lessened because of something done to him. The same recognition can—and should—be granted for all survivors.

Furthermore, what happened to Jesus cannot be dismissed as unimportant to the church or a 'distraction' from the church's concern for the gospel. Jesus and the cross are so central to Christian faith that it is impossible to deny the importance of his experience. Nor can Jesus be blamed for what was done to him. The common victim-blaming response is not readily available. Jesus cannot be faulted for provoking the sexual violence.

The negative responses to the *Folha* article show that when Jesus' experience of sexual violence is acknowledged, a common first reaction among Christian leaders or institutions is incredulity and negative judgement. Describing Jesus as a victim or survivor of sexual violence is denounced as mistaken, offensive, even blasphemous. However, these first reactions are regularly revised if the conversation around the reasons for seeing Jesus as a victim can be opened up and conducted in an appropriate pastoral manner. In the process of discussing Jesus' experience people often become more aware of the negative reactions of others, and they may also recognise negative reactions within themselves.

This process can help towards an understanding of secondary victimisation of survivors. The negative responses can be examined with questions that open up a wider perspective: 'Are these reactions indicative of negative attitudes towards survivors within the church?' 'Do we feel stigma and judgments of defilement even when we can rationalise that these are unjust?' Discussions of first responses to Jesus' experiences and a greater understanding of what is behind these can be one of the most effective ways within church settings of bringing to the surface latent stigma against survivors.

Attention to the stigma associated with sexual violence offers opportunities to go beyond care and compassion for survivors—important as these are—and open up conversations on church complicity with secondary victimisation. As Le Roux argues (2021, 186), focussing on Jesus' experience is relevant not just to survivors but important for the whole church. Attention to Jesus' experience debunks beliefs in the sinfulness of survivors, that they have lesser value, are not to be trusted, and are deserving of what happened. It provides a powerful example of Jesus the survivor who experienced sexual violence through no fault of his own, and who retains all his worth and dignity.

Dignity and Recovery

To speak of Jesus' experience of sexual violence is to confront the reality of his humiliation at a level that most people have not previously considered. From one perspective, a wish to avoid this is understandable. The cross has functioned in

Christian life as a focus of veneration and a promise of salvation: to imagine the cross as a site of unspeakable violence is difficult.

As the womanist theologian Delores Williams describes Jesus on the cross, he is 'the image of human sin in its most desecrated form'. She continues (Williams 1993, 166):

> This execution destroyed the body, but not before it mocked and defiled the Jewish man Jesus by publicly exposing his nakedness and private parts, by mocking the ministerial vision as they labelled him king of the Jews, by placing a crown of thorns upon his head mocking his dignity and the integrity of his divine mission.

Williams rejects the soteriological value of the cross and affirms that Christian hope rests in Jesus' life, not his death. She says: 'The cross thus becomes an image of defilement a gross manifestation of collective human sin. Jesus, then, does not conquer sin through death on the cross' (Williams 1993, 166).

Williams notes similarities between crucifixion and lynching as attacks on dignity (Williams 1993). In his book *The Cross and the Lynching Tree*, James Cone (2011) offers a powerful analysis of connections between these two degrading punishments. In 'He Never Said a Mumbalin' Word', Mitzi Smith has examined the connection between lynching and crucifixion further in their use of sexual violence against human dignity (Mitzi J. Smith 2021). Smith argues that lynching and crucifixion share a common purpose in targeting human dignity and a common approach in targeting sexual identity.

For crucifixion, the defilement of dignity is especially striking in the earliest artistic renderings of Jesus crucifixion (the Pereire magical gem and Palatine graffito discussed in Chapter 3). But from the fifth century onwards, when Christian artists started to show Jesus on the cross, this changed. In Christian art, Jesus was invariably shown wearing a loincloth on the cross, even though there is no loincloth mentioned in the text.

How should this loincloth be viewed in light of the argument in previous chapters? One option is to see the loincloth as a symbol of Christian denial. It can be viewed as an attempt to cover up the reality of abuse. Wil Gafney (2013) writes that the sexual abuse of Jesus 'is so traumatizing for the Church that we have covered it up—literally—covering Jesus' genitals on our crucifixes'. Seen in this way, the loincloth is an enduring symbol of the refusal to view the crucifixion scene with honesty and integrity. For most of Christian history this is an accurate judgement on how it has served. It has been part of a 'cover-up'. If this view is taken, the response to the loincloth might be to call for new images and artwork which are more honest and truthful in acknowledging abuse.

There is another option: creative reinterpretation. The social understanding of the loincloth might be reframed to acknowledge that it is imaginary device, but the impulse behind it is not to deny the truth but to restore and 'recover' dignity. When the Romans stripped and exposed Jesus, they sought to take away his dignity by uncovering and abusing his naked body. In response, the artistic convention of re-covering Jesus' nakedness by including an (imaginary) loincloth could be constructed as an appropriate and dignified response.

Andrew Graystone writes of the Good Samaritan's response to the man who fell among thieves on the road from Jerusalem to Jericho (Luke 10:25–37). His focus is on the meaning of the parable for the church in the context of sexual abuse. Graystone notices the element of stripping in the parable (Luke 10:30) which often receives little attention. If someone has been stripped, Graystone writes, the response should be a form of 're-dress' (2022, 13):

> What is the role of the church with victims of recent or non-recent abuse? I want to suggest that it is to reverse the dynamics of the trauma and thus 're-dress' the naked victim—to restore the personhood, dignity, and hope they have lost.

Graystone's belief that the church is called to reverse the dynamics of trauma through 're-dress' offers inspiration for a more positive interpretation of what Christian art has done in providing Jesus with a loincloth. The loincloth might be affirmed as a way to symbolically re-cover and re-dress Jesus, as a way to restore the dignity that was stripped in crucifixion. In this view, although the loincloth is not historical, it can nonetheless be recognised as an appropriate response (or at least a first step) in the restoration of personhood and dignity.

The words of the parable of judgement in Matthew 25:31–46 can provide further inspiration for this. This parable, often referred to as the parable of the sheep and the goats, calls for the clothing of the naked and all those in need. In the parable, Jesus (in the role of the king) speaks first to the righteous on his right hand. He tells of his times of need when they helped him. They offered food when he was hungry, water when thirsty, welcome as a stranger (Matt. 25:35). He says, 'I was naked and you gave me clothing, I was sick and you took care of me, I was in prison and you visited me' (Matt. 25:36). They ask him when they saw him hungry, or thirsty, or a stranger, and 'when was it that we saw you a stranger and welcomed you, or naked and gave you clothing?' (Matt. 25:38). To this Jesus replies: 'Truly I tell you, just as you did it to one of the least of these who are members of my family, you did it to me' (Matt. 25:41). To underline the point, and remove any doubt, Jesus then repeats the same message for those on his left hand (Matt. 25:42–45; Poole 2021, 82).

The location of the parable in Matthew 25 places it within Jesus' final days in Jerusalem. It brings Matthew 25 to an end, and Matthew 26 opens with the ominous warning that looks ahead to Matthew 27: 'When Jesus had finished saying all these things, he said to his disciples "You know that after two days the Passover is coming, and the Son of Man will be handed over to be crucified"' (Matt. 26:1–2). Although Jesus is fully clothed as he offers the parable in Matthew 25, it is only a matter of days before he will be crucified naked. Whilst the nakedness Jesus speaks about in Matthew 25 is in a context of poverty and destitution, there may also be here a discrete reference to his own imminent nakedness in crucifixion. The need for a response takes on a fuller meaning in the context of crucifixion:

'I was naked and you gave me clothing'. The loincloth can be reimagined as an appropriate response to crucifixion in light of these words.

However, the loincloth can only serve this helpful symbolic purpose of 'recovering' nakedness if it is also recognised as a creative response and not a historical fact. If it is mistakenly taken at face value as something Jesus had at the cross, or misunderstood as concealing something actually shameful, then the artistic convention of including the loincloth is worse than useless. It is only if the loincloth is viewed as an intentional artful addition that it is able to make this positive contribution. Rather than disguising or denying the stripping, the loincloth can then symbolise that Jesus' historical experience included forced nudity; this part of the story requires a response as signalled in the parable of judgement. The loincloth can then become an opportunity for both memory and action rather than amnesia and denial.

Resurrection

Understanding Jesus' experience can help the church to rethink how it sees those who experience sexual violence and to rethink its own complicity in secondary victimisation. The word 'repentance' is derived from 'rethinking'. The rethinking that the church is called to do on Jesus as a victim of sexual abuse can be theologically framed as a task of positive repentance. This also offers opportunities for rethinking in other areas of theology, including new thinking on resurrection (Heim 2019; Heim and Johnson 2020a, 2020b).

Paul goes out of his way to stress that the resurrection of Jesus was not just resurrection after death: it was a resurrection after crucifixion. Resurrection was not just a return to life; in the context of crucifixion, resurrection was a restoration of dignity and an affirmation of human worth in the face of degradation. Resurrection speaks of a profound transformation in the world.

Christ's resurrection was therefore an invitation for people to understand their lives and their relationship with God in new ways. In the old worldview, the shameful cross destroyed, diminished, and degraded the victim, and denied the victim any form of honour. The cross appeared as an insurmountable barrier and stumbling block, to undermine any claim that might be made in the name of Christ. But Paul came to see that everything changed when God raised Jesus from death on the cross. The humiliation of crucifixion was not a barrier for the proclamation of Jesus' life and message as good news. On the contrary, God's raising and restoring one who had been crucified was at the centre of the good news itself. If God stood in solidarity with victims—and even the crucified victim—and raised the crucified to life, this was a radical transformation of conventional values and social expectations. It made everything anew (2 Cor. 5:17).

Great care and sensitivity is needed for theological reflection on resurrection in the context of suffering if it is to make a positive difference to the church and its theology. Attention is needed to avoid what in Bonhoeffer's words might be described as 'cheap grace' (Bonhoeffer 1959, 45–60): an understanding of resurrection that is unaccountable to the reality of the cross and the lived experience of survivors. Above all, having faith in resurrection does not mean that what Jesus suffered in crucifixion is acceptable. The proclamation of resurrection is not a benign reassurance that despite the violence of the cross, everything is okay. Survivors of sexual abuse have spoken of the sense of alienation and frustration they feel when their experience of suffering is met by a glib claim that the resurrection offers reassurance that all is well.

There are difficult questions on how to understand Paul's view that God 'did not withhold his own Son but gave him up for all of us' (Rom 8.32). However, there is no question that in Paul's eyes, God raised the one crucified, and this showed that nothing could stand as barrier to God's love. As Paul says, 'Who will separate us from the love of Christ? Will hardship, or distress, or persecution, or famine, or nakedness, or peril, or sword? (Rom. 8.35). After citing Psalm 44:23 on suffering, Paul lists possible obstacles to the love of God and declares that Christ's death shows that none is sufficient:

> For I am convinced that neither death, nor life, nor angels, nor rulers, nor things present, nor things to come, nor powers, nor height, nor depth, nor anything else in all creation, will be able to separate us from the love of God in Christ Jesus our Lord.
>
> (Rom. 8.38–39)

In recent years I have worked with Rocío Figueroa to learn more about how survivors respond to seeing Jesus as a victim of sexual abuse (Figueroa and Tombs 2020, 2021, 2022). Some survivors find great solidarity and comfort in viewing Jesus as a fellow survivor. Others see Jesus' experience as so different to their own that little is to be gained from reflecting on his suffering. Others point out that Jesus was raised in just three days but that they have suffered years and sometimes decades without experiencing resurrection, renewal, or relief. One survivor told us that Jesus at least had a trial (Figueroa and Tombs 2020, 66). Some survivors will remain cautious of *any* attempt to reflect on what resurrection might mean in the context of sexual violence. It will take more time and many voices to wrestle with this challenge before any adequate response to these questions can start to take shape. Whatever the resurrection might offer towards a meaningful theological response to sexual abuse, it is not a promise of quick or easy answers.

The cautions and concerns expressed by survivors need to be heard. Shannel T. Smith (2021) offers a particularly evocative and thoughtful reflection on these issues. In our work, Figueroa and I also heard from survivors who fear that talk of Jesus as a victim might be appropriated by the church and used to negate rather than to acknowledge their suffering (Figueroa and Tombs 2021). To recognise the suffering of Jesus, and to speak of the church as the body of Christ, cannot be a way to distract from the bodily suffering of survivors. Nor should talk of resurrection suggest that crucifixion was anything other than it was: torture and cruelty. Attention to the meaning of resurrection is not to suggest that previous horror suddenly becomes unimportant, let alone benign, because it is part of a wider providential plan. There is no divine plan where the end (resurrection) justifies the means (crucifixion).

Moving forward too quickly to focus on resurrection is a mistake. The reality of what happened on the cross must be acknowledged and absorbed before there can be any meaningful discussion of what it means to proclaim resurrection. Churches are often reluctant to dwell on the suffering of Good Friday or the emptiness of Holy Saturday (Rambo 2010). The reassurance of resurrection is frequently read forward into the Good Friday story to give the cross a 'happy ending' and make the cross itself seem like something good. In this context, the name 'Good Friday' seems a misnomer; a different name such as Long Friday, Sorrowful Friday, or Desolate Friday may be more apt.[2] Resurrection is not a reward or compensation that makes the trauma of crucifixion bearable. The resurrection does not make the cross comfortable, nor does it take away the evil of the cross or 'solve' the problem of crucifixion.

For reasons of space, the soteriological issues that arise from interpreting the cross as part of a divine plan will need to be addressed elsewhere and as part of a wider conversation on the cross and violence. Feminist critiques of atonement models offer a powerful challenge to traditional ways of thinking about the cross and redemptive violence (Brown and Bohn 1989; Williams 1993; Brock and Parker 2001, 2008). These critiques apply all the more when the cross and the abuses which accompanied crucifixion are understood to include sexual violence.

Reflection on resurrection must recognise that the damage done by sexual violence cannot be undone. There is no way to turn the clock back and make what happened disappear. There are, however, some responses that might offer hope and healing rather than encourage hostile judgement or negative silence. Monica Poole writes: 'The narrative of resurrection is a narrative of restoration of honour and re-establishment of community connections' (Poole 2021). Poole notes that these are precisely the things that trauma specialist Judith Herman stresses in her article 'Justice from the Victim's Perspective' (Herman 2005). Two of the most helpful messages a church can offer to support this are 'you are not alone' and 'you are not to blame' (Wesley-Smith 2018; Tombs 2022).

'You are not alone': this has happened to others. At a cognitive level, survivors are all too aware that what happened to them has also happened to many others. Yet at the same time, it is common for survivors to report feeling isolated and alone. Awareness of what happened to Jesus can counter this sense of isolation. Knowing that one's experience is shared by others is not a solution to every problem, and some survivors may not find it helpful. But a sense of relationship and solidarity can reduce the sense of isolation. This often makes suffering easier to bear. One survivor explained how much this understanding of Jesus meant to her, because 'when I was abused, I never imagined that God could understand my shame' (Reaves and Tombs 2019, 411).[3]

The message that 'you are not to blame' is equally important. As discussed above, Jesus as a victim of sexual violence offers a counter-narrative to victim-blaming and stigma. The message 'you are not to blame' is a message that churches should offer to all victims of sexual violence, but often churches fail to make this clear. Reassurance that you are not to blame can make an enormous difference. It is not just a matter of survivors knowing this; it is also important to feel it. A survivor we interviewed explained that it helped her to see herself in a new way. At one level, she already knew her own innocence, but there are times when she is troubled by doubts and a temptation to self-blame:

> Despite saying to myself 'You are not guilty', one part of me, in my innermost part, maintains my guilt and leads me to accuse myself, 'You could have done something to avoid the abuse'.

She found that Jesus' experience offered her reassurance. She explained:

> And then I have the experience and the knowledge that Jesus was innocent. That makes it easier to believe that I am innocent. It has been a beginning. Reading it has been like a relief. It is not just on a theoretical level. There is an emotional level that helps me to go into my heart. I love Jesus. I don't blame him. I don't say to him, 'You had to do something. You could have avoided it'. Seeing his innocence, I see my innocence.
>
> (Figueroa and Tombs 2021, 296)

Conclusion

Studying accounts of torture, ancient and modern, and asking where the stripping, mocking, and crucifixion of Jesus should be located in relation to those accounts is disturbing and difficult, both as a writer and as a reader. What purpose is served by acknowledging the sexual violence of Jesus' crucifixion? Is any positive value to be found in such inquiry?

This book has been written in the belief that the unspeakable horror and shame associated with crucifixion need to be recognised but that they do not need to be the final word. There are biblical, theological, and pastoral aspects to the possible responses. For example, facing the brutality and indignity of crucifixion can lead the church to reflect on its response to sexual violence. It is an invitation to respond in ways that reaffirm the dignity of survivors and to reinforce the messages to those that experience abuse that 'you are not alone' and 'you are not to blame'. There are also opportunities to engage in new ways with an understanding of resurrection and with what it means for the church to be the body of Christ.

There are a number of convictions that have motivated the writing of this book, and in conclusion these may be summarised under three points (Tombs 2022, 97–98).

First, what is recorded in the text matters. The text in Mark 15:16–20 and Matthew 27:26–31 is clear and explicit, that Jesus was repeatedly stripped in a humiliating mockery involving about 500 soldiers and then displayed naked during crucifixion to die in front of a hostile crowd. Recognising this, and using the frank language of 'sexual abuse', will make a difference to how we think about the text and how we think about Jesus. As the study discusses, there may also have been further sexualised abuse in the mocking and crucifixion, but this is not clear, and it cannot be judged conclusively from the available evidence. Even so, the stripping and enforced nudity discussed in Chapter 1 provided a compelling reason to conclude that Jesus was a victim of sexual abuse.

Second, recognising sexual abuse matters. In comparison to when this argument was presented over 20 years ago, there is now much greater public awareness of sexual abuse as a problem in society and in churches. There is also more awareness that sexual abuses can sometimes be 'hidden in plain sight' (Tombs 2020b). Evidence which should give cause for concern is often minimised or dismissed as unimportant. Abusers can readily take advantage of this to continue their abuse. The widespread failure to see the stripping of Jesus as sexual abuse shows how easy it is to miss clear evidence of sexual abuse, even when the evidence should be obvious and in plain sight. Likewise, the failure to even ask what else might have happened shows an lack of imagination on the part of churches. The churches, and especially church leaders and anyone involved in safeguarding, should take lessons from how the sexual abuse of Jesus has gone unrecognised and unacknowledged for so long.

Third, responding to sexual abuse matters. In many conversations about the work over the years there has been resistance to thinking of Jesus as a victim of sexual abuse. The reasons for this are varied and are not always explicitly articulated. However, through conversations over the years, a common element in negative reactions is the feeling that shame and stigma would attach to Jesus if he is seen in this way. There is a fear that Jesus would be lessened, disgraced, or demeaned if it is true that he was subjected to sexual abuse.

The work gives churches an opportunity to explore and challenge the assumptions behind these harmful perceptions. Care needs to be taken that this is done in ways that are sensitive and appropriate, of course. But that is true of any difficult issue. Discussing Jesus' experience of abuse can help bring to the surface negative attitudes to those who experience abuse. An effective pastoral response should challenge and change these perceptions. It can help survivors. It can also help churches to be more true to their identity as the body of Christ.

A commitment to the truth, and to seeing the cross for what it is, can be painful. It can also offer new freedom. The Gospel of John speaks of the liberating potential of truth. 'You will know the truth, and the truth will make you free' (John 8:32). There are at least two implications to what the Gospel writer says. First, truth is not a threat to be feared but a gift to be embraced. Second, a central task of the church is to seek and tell the truth. Even when truth is difficult or disruptive—and perhaps especially then—a commitment to seek it, and tell it, can offer a pathway to freedom and new life.

Notes

1 As West explains, these Bible studies are living documents that are constantly revised and renewed (West 2022). This sequence of questions was the third version of

a Bible study on Matthew 27:26–31 and was developed during a research collaboration in 2019.
2 It has been suggested that the term 'Good Friday' is derived from 'God's Friday', but this derivation appears to be unfounded; see Wickman (2019).
3 Neafsey writes (2014, 10): 'Paradoxically, the fact that Jesus was tortured can be a source of consolation to some torture survivors, who are able to experience, through him, something of what it feels like to be empathically understood or known'.

Bibliography

Adams, Sean A. 2008. 'Crucifixion in the Ancient World: A Response to L.L. Welborn', in Stanley E. Porter (ed.), *Paul's World*. Leiden: Brill.
Aguilar, Mario. 2015. *Religion, Torture and the Liberation of God*. London: Routledge.
Allegra, Cécile. 2017. 'Revealed: Male Rape Used Systematically in Libya as Instrument of War', *The Guardian* (3 November).
Anjos, Márvio dos. 2022, 'Corpo, cruz e abuso', *Folha de S.Paulo* (10 April 2022), ilustríssima: C8-C9.
Archdiocese of Sao Paulo. 1986. *Torture in Brazil: A Report by the Archdiocese of São Paulo*. New York: Vintage Books (Portuguese orig. 1985).
Asikainen, Susanna. 2018. *Jesus and Other Men: Ideal Masculinities in the Synoptic Gospels*. Leiden: Brill.
Barbet, Pierre. 1953. *A Doctor at Calvary: The Passion of Our Lord Jesus Christ as Described by a Surgeon*. New York: Doubleday.
Begg, Moazzam. 2006. *Enemy Combatant: My Imprisonment at Guantanamo, Bagram and Kandahar*. New York: New Press.
Belser, Julia Watts. 2014. 'Sex in the Shadow of Rome: Sexual Violence and Theological Lament in Talmudic Disaster Tales', *Journal of Feminist Studies in Religion* 30 (1): 5–24.
Bergsma, John Sietze, and Scott Walker Hahn. 2005. 'Noah's Nakedness and the Curse on Canaan (Genesis 9:20–27)', *Journal of Biblical Literature* 124 (1): 25–40.
Blyth, Caroline, Emily Colgan, and Katie Edwards, eds. 2018. *Rape Culture, Gender Violence and Religion: Biblical Perspectives*. London: Palgrave Macmillan.
Bolsonaro, Michelle. 2022. (11 April); https://twitter.com/MiBolsonaro/status/1513411477 650255872 (account currently suspended).
Bonhoeffer, Dietrich. 1959. *The Cost of Discipleship*. London: SCM Press, rev edn (German orig. 1937).
Boyarin, Daniel. 1993. *Carnal Israel: Reading Sex in Talmudic Culture*. Berkeley: University of California Press.
Brock, Rita Nakashima, and Rebecca Ann Parker. 2001. *Proverbs of Ashes: Violence, Redemptive Suffering and the Search for What Saves Us*. Boston: Beacon Press.
Brock, Rita Nakashima, and Rebecca Ann Parker. 2008. *Saving Paradise: How Christianity Traded Love of This World for Crucifixion and Empire*. Boston: Beacon Press.
Brown, Joanne Carlson, and Carole R. Bohn, eds. 1989. *Christianity, Patriarchy and Abuse: A Feminist Critique*. Cleveland, OH: Pilgrim Press.
Brown, Raymond E. 1994. *Death of the Messiah*. New York: Doubleday.

Brownmiller, Susan. 1975. *Against Our Will: Men, Women and Rape*. New York: Simon & Schuster.

Burgess-Jackson, Keith. 1999. *A Most Detestable Crime: New Philosophical Essays on Rape*. Oxford: Oxford University Press.

Cavanaugh, William T. 1998. *Torture and Eucharist: Theology, Politics and the Body of Christ*. Oxford: Blackwell.

Channel 4 News. 2011. 'Gaddafi Buried at Dawn in "Secret" Location', (25 October); www.channel4.com/news/gaddafi-buried-at-dawn-in-secret-location

Chapman, Cynthia R. 2004. *The Gendered Language of Warfare in the Israelite-Assyrian Encounter*. Winona Lake, IN: Eisenbrauns.

Chapman, David W. 2008. *Ancient Jewish and Christian Perceptions of Crucifixion*. WUNT 244. Tübingen: Mohr Siebeck.

Chapman, David W., and Eckhard J. Schnabel. 2015. *The Trial and Crucifixion of Jesus*. WUNT 344. Tübingen: Mohr Siebeck.

Christie, Nils. 1986. 'The Perfect Victim', in Ezzat A. Fattah (ed.), *From Crime Policy to Victim Policy*. New York: Palgrave Macmillan: 17–30.

Coleman, Kathleen M. 1990. 'Fatal Charades: Roman Executions Staged as Mythological Enactments', *Journal of Roman Studies* 80: 44–73.

Coleman, Kathleen M. 2018. 'The Fragility of Evidence: Torture in Ancient Rome', in Scott A. Anderson and Martha C. Nussbaum (eds.), *Confronting Torture: Essays on the Ethics, Legality, History, and Psychology of Torture Today*. Chicago: University of Chicago Press.

Colgan, Emily, and Caroline Blyth, eds. 2022. *Accompanying Survivors of Sexual Harm: A Toolkit for Churches*. Shiloh Project.

CONADEP [National Commission on Disappeared People]. 1986. *Nunca Mas (Never Again)*. London: Faber and Faber (Spanish orig. 1984).

Cone, James H. 2011. *The Cross and the Lynching Tree*. Maryknoll, NY: Orbis Books.

Cone, James H. 2018. *Said I Wasn't Gonna Tell Nobody: The Making of a Black Theologian*. Maryknoll, NY: Orbis Books.

Conway, Colleen M. 2008. *Behold the Man: Jesus and Greco-Roman Masculinity*. Oxford: Oxford University Press.

Cook, John Granger. 2014. *Crucifixion in the Mediterranean World*. WUNT 327. Tübingen: Mohr Siebeck.

Danner, Mark. 2004. *Torture and Truth: America, Abu Ghraib, and the War on Terror*. New York: New York Review of Books.

Dawson, Rosie. 2021a. 'Jesus as a Victim of Sexual Abuse', *Shiloh Project Podcast Interview with David Tombs* (24 March); https://open.spotify.com/episode/6098pBFuFSrQA2r1eufdoI?nd=1

Dawson, Rosie. 2021b. 'Was Jesus Sexually Abused?', *Church Times* (1 April); www.churchtimes.co.uk/articles/2021/1-april/features/features/was-jesus-sexually-abused

Deacy, Susan, and Karen F. Pierce, eds. 1997. *Rape in Antiquity: Sexual Violence in the Greek and Roman Worlds*. London: Duckworth.

Dolan, Chris. 2018. 'Victims Who are Men', in Fionnuala Ní Aoláin, Naomi Cahn, and Dina Haynes (eds.), *The Oxford Handbook of Gender and Conflict*. Oxford: Oxford University Press.

Dover, Kenneth J. 1978. *Greek Homosexuality*. Cambridge, MA: Harvard University Press.

Du Toit, Louise, and Elisabet le Roux. 2020. 'Feminist Reflection on Male Victims of Conflict Related Sexual Violence', *European Journal of Women's Studies* 28 (2): 115–128.

Easton, Martha. 2006. 'The Wound of Christ, the Mouth of Hell: Appropriations and Inversions of Female Anatomy in the Later Middle Ages', in Susan L'Engle and Gerald B. Guest (eds.), *Tributes to Jonathan J.G. Alexander: The Making and Meaning of Illuminated Medieval and Renaissance Manuscripts, Art and Architecture*. London: Harvey Miller: 395–414.

Edwards, Katie B., and David Tombs. 2018. '#HimToo—Why Jesus Should be Recognised as a Victim of Sexual Violence', *The Conversation* (23 March); https://theconversation.com/himtoo-why-jesus-should-be-recognised-as-a-victim-of-sexual-violence-93677

Edwards, William D. 1986. 'On the Physical Death of Jesus Christ', *Journal of the American Medical Association* 255: 1455–1463.

Ehrman, Bart D., and Zlatko Pleše. 2011. *The Apocryphal Gospels: Texts and Translations*. Oxford: Oxford University Press.

Evans, Craig. 2017. 'Graffiti', in Tom Thatcher, Chris Keith, Raymond F. Person Jr., and Elsie R. Stern (eds.), *The Dictionary of the Bible and Ancient Media*. London: Bloomsbury: 160–161.

Figueroa, Rocío, and David Tombs. 2020. 'Recognising Jesus as a Victim of Sexual Abuse: Responses from Sodalicio Survivors in Peru', *Religion and Gender* 10 (1): 57–75; https://doi.org/10.1163/18785417-01001003.

Figueroa, Rocío, and David Tombs. 2021. 'Seeing His Innocence, I See My Innocence', in Jayme R. Reaves, David Tombs and Rocío Figueroa (eds.), *When Did We See You Naked?: Jesus as a Victim of Sexual Abuse*. London: SCM Press: 287–312.

Figueroa, Rocío, and David Tombs. 2022. 'Living in Obedience and Suffering in Silence: The Shattered Faith of Nuns Abused by Priests', in Mathias Wirth, Isabelle Noth, and Silvia Schroer (eds.), *Sexualisierte Gewalt in kirchlichen Kontexten: Neue interdisziplinäre Perspektiven* [Sexual Violence in the Context of the Church: New Interdisciplinary Perspectives]. Berlin: De Gruyter: 45–74.

Finney, Mark T. 2013. 'Servile Supplicium: Shame and the Deuteronomic Curse—Crucifixion in Its Cultural Context', *Biblical Theology Bulletin* 43 (3): 124–134.

Forrest, Duncan, ed. 1996. *A Glimpse of Hell: Reports on Torture Worldwide*. London: Cassell and Amnesty International.

Fredrick, David. 1997. 'Reading Broken Skin: Violence in Roman Elegy', in Judith Hallet and Marilyn Skinner (eds.), *Roman Sexualities*. Princeton: Princeton University Press: 172–193.

Fulda, Herman. 1878. *Das Kreuz und die Kreuzigung. Eine antiquarische Untersuchung*. Breslau: Wilhelm Koebner.

Gaca, Kathy L. 2018. 'The Martial Rape of Girls and Women in Antiquity and Modernity', in Fionnuala Ní Aoláin, Naomi Cahn, Dina Francesca Haynes, and Nahla Valji (eds.), *The Oxford Handbook of Gender and Conflict*. Oxford: Oxford University Press: 305–315.

Gafney, Wil. 2013. 'Crucifixion and Sexual Violence', *HuffPost* (28 March); https://huffpost.netblogpro.com/entry/crucifixion-and-sexual-violence_b_2965369

Ganzevoort, Ruard, and Srdjan Sremac. 2016. 'Masculinity, Spirituality, and Male Wartime Sexual Trauma', in Yochai Ataria, David Gurevitz, Haviva Pedaya, and Yuval Neria (eds.), *Interdisciplinary Handbook of Trauma and Culture*. Cham, Switzerland: Springer: 339–351.

Glancy, Jennifer. 2002. *Slavery in Early Christianity*. Oxford: Oxford University Press.

Goffman, Erving. 1963. *Stigma: Notes on the Management of Spoiled Identity*. New York: Simon & Schuster.

Golden, Renny, and Michael McConnell. 1986. *Sanctuary: The New Underground Railway*. Maryknoll, NY: Orbis Books.

Gourevitch, Philip, and Errol Morris. 2008. *Standard Operating Procedure: A War Story*. New York: Penguin Press.

Gqola, Pumla Dineo. 2015. *Rape: A South African Nightmare*. Johannesburg: MFBooks Joburg.

Graystone, Andrew. 2022. *Falling Among Thieves: Understanding and Responding to Church-Related Abuse*. Rochdale, UK: William Temple Foundation.

Graziano, Franz. 1992. *Divine Violence: Spectacle, Psychosexuality, and Radical Christianity in the Argentine 'Dirty War'*. Oxford: Westview Press.

Greenough, Chris. 2021. *The Bible and Sexual Violence Against Men*. Abingdon, Oxon: Routledge.

Gutierrez, Gustavo. 1981. *A Theology of Liberation: History, Politics and Salvation*. London: SCM Press (Spanish orig. 1971; ET 1973).

Hallett, Judith P., and Marilyn Skinner, eds. 1997. *Roman Sexualities*. Princeton, NJ: Princeton University Press.

Harley-McGowan, Felicity. 2019a. 'Jesus the Magician? A Crucifixion Amulet and Its Date', in Kata Endreffy, Árpád M. Nagy, and Jeffrey Spier (eds.), *Magical Gems in Their Contexts*. Rome: L'Erma di Bretschneider: 103–116.

Harley-McGowan, Felicity. 2019b. 'The Alexamenos Graffito', in Chris Keith, Helen Bond, and Jens Schröter (eds.), *The Reception of Jesus in the First Three Centuries*. London: Bloomsbury T&T Clark: 105–139.

Heath, Elaine A. 2011. *We Were the Least of These: Reading the Bible with Survivors of Sexual Abuse*. Grand Rapids, MI: Brazos.

Heim, Erin. 2019. 'Resurrection and the #MeToo Movement: A Constructive Reading of the Resurrected Body in First Corinthians 15: 35–49', Paper presented at University of Edinburgh (27 September).

Heim, Erin, and Dru Johnson. 2020a. 'Resurrection and the #MeToo Movement: Part 1', *OnScript Podcast* 90 (16 June); https://onscript.study/podcast/erin-heim-with-dru-johnson-resurrection-and-the-metoo-movement-part-1/

Heim, Erin, and Dru Johnson. 2020b. 'Resurrection and the #Metoo Movement: Part 2', *OnScript Podcast* 99 (6 October); https://onscript.study/podcast/erin-heim-resurrection-and-the-metoo-movement-part-ii/

Hemker, Julia. 1985. 'Rape and the Founding of Rome', *Helios* 12: 9–20.

Hengel, Martin. 1977. *Crucifixion: In the Ancient World and the Folly of the Message of the Cross*. London: SCM Press (German orig. 1976).

Herman, Judith. 1997. *Trauma and Recovery*. New York: Basic Books.

Herman, Judith. 2005. 'Justice from the Victim's Perspective', *Violence Against Women* 11 (5): 571–602.

Hersh, Seymour M. 2004. *Chain of Command: The Road from 9/11 to Abu Ghraib*. New York: HarperCollins.

HRW (Human Rights Watch). 2012. *Death of a Dictator: Bloody Vengeance in Sirte*. New York: Human Rights Watch, 2012.

Hurtado, Larry. 2013. 'The Staurogram: The Earliest Depiction of Jesus' Crucifixion', *Biblical Archaeological Society* 39 (2): 49–52.

Jensen, Robin Margaret. 2012. 'Nudity in Early Christian Art', in Auou Cissé Niang, and Carolyn Osiek (eds.), *Text, Image, and Christians in the Graeco-Roman World: A Festschrift in Honor of David Lee Balch*. Eugene, OR: Pickwick.

Key, David. 2021. 'Crucifixion was Practised in Roman Britain, New Evidence Reveals', *Independent* (8 December).

Knox, Robert. 1681. *An Historical Relation of the Island Ceylon in the East Indies*. London: Richard Chiswell (Project Gutenberg ebook, 2004); www.gutenberg.org/files/14346/14346-h/14346-h.htm

Kotansky, Roy D. 2017. 'The Magic "Crucifixion Gem" in the British Museum', *Greek, Roman, and Byzantine Studies* 57: 631–659.

Kyle, Donald G. 1998. *Spectacles of Death in Ancient Rome*. New York: Routledge.

Lamb, Christina. 2020. *Our Bodies, Their Battlefield: What War Does to Women*. London: William Collins.

Langlands, Rebecca. 2006. *Sexual Morality in Ancient Rome*. Cambridge: Cambridge University Press.

Lemos, Tracy M. 2006. 'Shame and Mutilation of Enemies', *Journal of Biblical Literature* 125 (2): 225–241.

Le Roux, Elisabet. 2014. *The Role of African Christian Churches in Dealing with Sexual Violence Against Women: The case of the Democratic Republic of Congo, Rwanda and Liberia*. Unpublished PhD thesis, University of Stellenbosch.

Le Roux, Elisabet. 2021. 'Jesus is a Survivor', in Jayme R. Reaves, David Tombs, and Rocío Figueroa (eds.), *When Did We See You Naked?: Jesus as a Victim of Sexual Abuse*. London: SCM Press: 178–194.

Le Roux, Elisabet et al. 2020. 'Engaging with Faith Groups to Prevent VAWG in Conflict-Affected Communities: Results From Two Community Surveys in the DRC', *BMC International Health and Human Rights*: 20–27; https://doi.org/10.1186/s12914-020-00246-8

Lightfoot, J.B. 1907. *The Apostolic Fathers*. New York: Macmillan.

Lipsi, Iusti (Justus Lipsius). 1606. *De Cruce: Libri tres: Ad sacram profanamque historiam utiles: Una cum Notts*. Antverpiae: Officiana Plantiniana, Apud Viduam et Ioannem Moretum (orig. 1594).

Luz, Ulrich. 2005. *Matthew 21–28: A Commentary*. Minneapolis: Fortress Press (German orig. 1989).

Mackey, Chris, and Greg Miller. 2004. *The Interrogators: Inside the Secret War Against al Qaeda*. New York: Little, Brown.

Mackie, Carolyn. 2021. 'Review: When Did We See You Naked?', *Women in Theology* (4 August); https://womenintheology.org/2021/08/03/review-when-did-we-see-you-naked/

Madigan, Lee, and Nancy Gamble. 1989. *The Second Rape: Society's Continued Betrayal of the Victim*. New York: Lexington Books.

Melanchthon, Monica, and Robyn Whitaker, eds. 2021. *Terror in the Bible: Rhetoric, Gender, and Violence*. International Voices in Biblical Studies Series. Atlanta, GA: SBL Press.

Melito of Sardis. 1979. *On Pascha and Fragments*. Trans. and ed. Stuart George Hall. Oxford: Clarendon Press.

Menéndez-Antuña, Luis. 2022. 'The Book of Torture: The Gospel of Mark, Crucifixion, and Trauma', *Journal of the American Academy of Religion* 90 (2): 377–395.

Moore, Stephen, and Janice Capel Anderson, eds. 2003. *New Testament Masculinities*. Semeia Studies. Atlanta, GA: Society of Biblical Literature.

Neafsey, John. 2014. *Crucified People: The Suffering of the Tortured in Today's World*. Maryknoll, NY: Orbis Books.

Nguyen, Nghiem L. 2006. 'Roman Rape: An Overview of Roman Rape Laws from the Republican Period to Justinian's Reign', *Michigan Journal of Gender and Law* 13 (1): 75–112.

Ní Aoláin, Fionnuala. 2016. 'Forced Nudity: What International Law and Practice Tell Us', *Just Security*; www.justsecurity.org/31325/forced-nudity-international-law-practice/

Nidditch, Susan. 1993. *War in the Hebrew Bible: A Study in the Ethics of Violence*. Oxford: Oxford University Press.

O'Collins, Gerald G. 1992.'Crucifixion' in David Noel Freedman (ed.), *The Anchor Bible Dictionary*. Vol 1; New York: Doubleday: 1207–1211.

O'Donnell, Karen. 2021. 'Surviving Trauma at the Foot of the Cross', in Jayme R. Reaves, David Tombs, and Rocío Figueroa (eds.), *When Did We See You Naked?: Jesus as a Victim of Sexual Abuse*. London: SCM Press: 260–277.

Office of the Prosecutor, International Criminal Court. 2014. 'Policy Paper on Sexual and Gender-Based Crimes'; www.icc-cpi.int/sites/default/files/iccdocs/otp/Policy_Paper_on_Sexual_and_Gender-Based_Crimes-20_June_2014-ENG.pdf

Peel, Michael et al. 2000. 'The Sexual Abuse of Men in Detention in Sri Lanka', *Lancet* 355 (9220): 2069–2070.

Peters, Edward. 1996. *Torture*. Philadelphia: University of Pennsylvania Press, rev edn (orig. 1985).

Poole, Monica C. 2021. 'Family Resemblance: Reading Post-Crucifixion Encounters as Community Responses to Sexual Violence', in Jayme R. Reaves, David Tombs, and R. Figueroa (eds.), *When Did We See You Naked?: Jesus as a Victim of Sexual Abuse*. London: SCM Press: 67–90.

Punt, Jeremy. 2021.'Knowing Christ Crucified (1 Corinthians 2:2): Cross, Humiliation and Humility', in Jayme R. Reaves, David Tombs and Rocío Figueroa (eds.), *When Did We See You Naked?': Jesus as a Victim of Sexual Abuse*. London: SCM Press: 91–109.

Porciuncula, André. 2022. (11 April); https://twitter.com/andreporci/status/1513162206564823046 (Google translation).

Radner, Karen. 2015. 'High Visibility Punishment and Deterrent: Impalement in Assyrian Warfare and Legal Practice', *Journal for Ancient Near Eastern and Biblical Law* 21: 103–128.

Rambo, Shelly. 2010. *Spirit and Trauma: A Theology of Remaining*. Louisville, KY: Westminster John Knox Press.

Reaves, Jayme R., and David Tombs. 2019. '#MeToo Jesus: Naming Jesus as a Victim of Sexual Abuse', *International Journal of Public Theology* 13 (4): 387–412; https://doi.org/10.1163/15697320-12341588

Reaves, Jayme R., David Tombs, and Rocío Figueroa, eds. 2021. *When Did We See You Naked?: Jesus as a Victim of Sexual Abuse*. London: SCM Press.

Reeder, Caryn. 2017. 'Wartime Rape, the Romans, and the First Jewish Revolt', *Journal for the Study of Judaism* 48: 363–385.

Relman, Eliza. 2016. 'Pentagon Releases 198 Abuse Photos in Long-Running Lawsuit. What They Don't Show Is a Bigger Story', *ACLU National Security Project*; www.aclu.org/blog/national-security/torture/pentagon-releases-198-abuse-photos-long-running-lawsuit-what-they

REMHI (Recovery of History Memory Project). 1999. *Guatemala: Never Again!* Maryknoll, NY: Orbis Books.

Rhiannon, Graybill. 2021. *Texts after Terror: Rape, Sexual Violence, and the Hebrew Bible*. Oxford: Oxford University Press.

Roberts, Alexander, and James Donaldson, eds. 1885–96. *The Ante-Nicene Fathers: Translations of the Writings of the Fathers Down to AD 325*. Buffalo, NY: Christian Literature.

Samuelsson, Gunnar. 2011. *Crucifixion in Antiquity: An Inquiry into the Background of New Testament Terminology*. WUNT 310. Tübingen: Mohr Siebeck.

Sands, Phillipe. 2004. 'Stress, Hooding, Noise, Nudity, Dogs', *The Guardian* (19 April).

Scarsella, Hilary. 2020. 'Bearing Witness to Jesus, Resurrected Survivor of Sexual Violence', in Elizabeth Soto Albrecht and Darryl W. Stephens (eds.), *Liberating the Politics of Jesus*. London: T&T Clark: 151–166.
Schulz, Philipp. 2016. 'Transitional Justice for Male Victims of Conflict-Related Sexual and Gender-Based Violence', *International Journal of Rule of Law, Transitional Justice and Human Rights* 39: 39–50.
Schulz, Philipp. 2021. *Male Survivors of Wartime Sexual Violence: Perspectives from Northern Uganda*. Oakland: University of California Press.
Segovia, Fernando F. 2018. 'Jesus as Victim of State Terror: A Critical Reflection Twenty Years Later' in David Tombs, *Crucifixion, State Terror, and Sexual Abuse: Text and Context*. Dunedin, NZ: University of Otago, Centre for Theology and Public Issues: 22–31.
Sivakumaran, Sandesh. 2007. 'Sexual Violence Against Men in Armed Conflict', *European Journal of International Law* 18 (2): 253–276.
Sjoberg, Laura. 2014. *Gender, War and Conflict*. Cambridge: Polity.
Sjöholm, Maria. 2017. 'Forced Nudity', in *Gender-Sensitive Norm Interpretation by Regional Human Rights Law Systems*. Leiden: Brill: 345–361.
Smith, Christian. 1996. *Resisting Reagan: The U.S. Central America Peace Movement*. Chicago: University of Chicago Press.
Smith, Mitzi J. 2021. '"He Never Said a Mumbalin' Word": A Womanist Perspective of Crucifixion, Sexual Violence and Sacralized Silence', in Jayme R. Reaves, David Tombs, and Rocío Figueroa (eds.), *When Did We See You Naked?: Jesus as a Victim of Sexual Abuse*. London: SCM Press: 110–128.
Smith, Shanell T. 2021. 'This Is My Body: A Womanist Reflection on Jesus' Sexualized Trauma During His Crucifixion from a Survivor of Sexual Assault', in Jayme R. Reaves, David Tombs, and Rocío Figueroa (eds.), *When Did We See You Naked?: Jesus as a Victim of Sexual Abuse*. London: SCM Press: 278–286.
Sobrino, Jon. 1994. *The Principle of Mercy: Taking the Crucified People from the Cross*. Maryknoll, NY: Orbis Books.
Steinberg, Leo. 1983. *The Sexuality of Christ in Renaissance Art and in Modern Oblivion*. Cambridge, MA: MIT Press (October–Summer).
Stiebert, Johanna. 2019. *Rape Myths, the Bible, and #MeToo*. Abingdon, Oxon: Routledge, 2019.
Stone, Ken. 1996. *Sex, Honor and Power in the Deuteronomistic History*. Sheffield, UK: Sheffield Academic Press.
Stratton, Kimberly B. 2019. 'Violence', in Benjamin H. Dunning (ed.), *The Oxford Handbook of New Testament, Gender, and Sexuality*. Oxford: Oxford University Press: 607–626.
Tabeling, Adam. 2020. 'Martial Valor of the Roman Emperors as Divinity on the Sebasteion at Aphrodisias', *Chronika, Institute for European and Mediterranean Archaeology* 10: 82–93.
Taylor, Jonathan B. 2008. *Crucifixion*. New York: History Channel.
Tearfund. 2011. *Silent No More: The Untapped Potential of the Worldwide Church in Addressing Sexual Violence*. Teddington, UK: Tearfund.
Thiede, Barbara. 2022. *Rape Culture in the House of David: A Company of Men*. Abingdon, Oxon: Routledge.
Tombs, David. 1995. 'The Hermeneutics of Liberation', in Stanley E. Porter and David Tombs (eds.), *Approaches to New Testament Study*. Sheffield, UK: Sheffield Academic Press: 310–355.

Bibliography

Tombs, David. 1999. 'Crucifixion, State Terror, and Sexual Abuse', *Union Seminary Quarterly Review* 53: 89–109; https://doi.org/10.7916/d8-wypm-vt48

Tombs, David. 2002a. *Latin American Liberation Theology*. Boston: Brill.

Tombs, David. 2002b. 'Honour, Shame, and Conquest: Male Identity, Sexual Violence and the Body Politic', *Journal of Hispanic/Latino Theology* 9 (4): 21–40.

Tombs, David. 2004. *Unspeakable Violence*. Unpublished PhD dissertation, University of London.

Tombs, David. 2006. 'Unspeakable Violence: The Truth Commissions in El Salvador and Guatemala', in Iain Maclean (ed.), *Reconciliation: Nations and Churches in Latin America*. Aldershot, UK: Ashgate: 55–84.

Tombs, David. 2009. 'Prisoner Abuse: From Abu Ghraib to *The Passion of the Christ*', in Linda Hogan, and Dylan Lehrke (eds.), *Religions and the Politics of Peace and Conflict*. Princeton Theological Monograph Series. Eugene, OR: Pickwick: 175–201.

Tombs, David. 2014. 'Silent No More: Sexual Violence in Conflict as a Challenge to the Worldwide Church', *Acta Theologica* 34 (2): 142–165; https://doi.org/10.4314/actat.v34i2.9

Tombs, David. 2015. *The Ongoing Legacy of Liberation Theology*. Inaugural Professorial Lecture. University of Otago (8 September); www.otago.ac.nz/cs/groups/public/@otagopodcast/documents/audio_video/otag

Tombs, David. 2018. *Crucifixion, State Terror, and Sexual Abuse: Text and Context*. Dunedin, NZ: University of Otago, Centre for Theology and Public Issues; http://hdl.handle.net/10523/8558.

Tombs, David. 2019. 'How Recognising Jesus as a Victim of Sexual Abuse Might Help Shift Catholic Culture', *The Conversation* (13 March); https://theconversation.com/how-recognising-jesus-as-a-victim-of-sexual-abuse-might-help-shift-catholic-culture-112754

Tombs, David. 2020a. 'Unspeakable Things: Drawing upon the Nanjing Massacre to Read Crucifixion as an Assault on Human Dignity', in Zhibin Xie, Pauline Kollontai, and Sebastian Kim (eds.), *Human Dignity, Human Rights, and Social Justice: A Chinese Interdisciplinary Dialogue with Global Perspectives*. Singapore: Springer.

Tombs, David. 2020b. 'Hidden in Plain Sight: Seeing the Stripping of Jesus as Sexual Violence', *Journal for Interdisciplinary Biblical Studies* Special Issue: Activism in the Biblical Studies Classroom: Global Perspectives 2 (1) (Autumn): 224–247; https://dx.doi.org/10.17613/ek9a-mx94

Tombs, David. 2021. 'Reading Crucifixion Narratives as Texts of Terror', in Monica Melanchthon, and Robyn Whitaker (eds.), *Terror in the Bible: Rhetoric, Gender, and Violence*. Atlanta, GA: SBL Press: 139–160.

Tombs, David. 2022. 'Asking the Right Questions: Noticing and Naming Sexual Abuse', Jione Havea, Emily Colgan and Nasili Vaka'uta (eds.), *Theology as Threshold: Invitations from Aotearoa New Zealand*. Lanham MD: Lexington Books / Fortress Academic: 85–105.

Trainor, Michael. 2014. *The Body of Jesus and Sexual Abuse: How the Gospel Passion Narrative Informs a Pastoral Approach*. Melbourne: Morning Star.

Trexler, Richard C. 1993. 'Gendering Christ Crucified', in Brendan Cassidy (ed.), *Iconography at the Crossroads*. Princeton, NJ: Department of Art and Archaeology, Princeton University.

Trexler, Richard C. 1995. *Sex and Conquest: Gendered Violence, Political Order and the European Conquest of the Americas*. Ithaca, NY: Cornell University Press.

Trible, Phyllis. 1984. *Texts of Terror: Literary-Feminist Readings of Biblical Narratives*. Overtures to Biblical Theology. Philadelphia: Fortress Press.

Tzaferis, Vassilios. 1985. 'Crucifixion—The Archaeological Evidence', *Biblical Archaeology Society* 11 (1): 44–53.

Ujamaa Centre. 2019. *A Contextual Bible Study on the Crucifixion of Jesus: Engaging the Issue of Male Violence Against Men*. Pietermaritzburg, South Africa: Ujamaa Centre; http://hdl.handle.net/10523/10233

Vogelzang, M.E., and M.J. van Bekkum. 1986. 'Meaning and Symbolism of Clothing in Ancient Near Eastern Texts', in H.L.J. Vanstiphout et al. (eds.), *Scripta Signa Vocis, Studies About Scripts, Scriptures, Scribes, and Languages in the Near East*. Groningen: Forsten: 265–282.

Walters, Jonathan. 1997. 'Invading the Roman Body: Manliness and Impenetrability in Roman Thought', in Judith P. Hallett and Marilyn B. Skinner (eds.), *Roman Sexualities*. Princeton, NJ: Princeton University Press: 29–43.

Wesley-Smith, Mike. 2018. 'Psychiatrist and Abuse Survivor to Victims: "You Are Not Alone and It's Not Your Fault"', *Newshub* (3 March); www.newshub.co.nz/home/shows/2018/03/psychiatrist-and-abuse-survivor-to-victims-you-are-not-alone-and-it-s-not-your-fault.html.

West, Gerald O. 2021. 'Jesus, Joseph, and Tamar Stripped: Trans-textual and Intertextual Resources for Engaging Sexual Violence Against Men', in Jayme R. Reaves, David Tombs, and Rocío Figueroa (eds.), *When Did We See You Naked?: Jesus as a Victim of Sexual Abuse*. London: SCM Press: 110–128.

West, Gerald O. 2022. 'Mobilizing Matthew among the Marginalized: Thirty Years of Community-based Bible Study in South Africa', *Currents in Theology and Mission*, 49 (4): 27–35.

Wickman, Forrest. 2019. 'Why Is Good Friday Called "Good Friday"?', *Slate* (19 April); https://slate.com/culture/2017/04/why-is-good-friday-called-good-friday-the-etymology-and-origins-of-the-holidays-name.html

Wigg Stevenson, Natalie. 2022. 'Review of When Did We See You Naked? Jesus as a Victim of Sexual Abuse', *Studies in Christian Ethics* 35 (3): 668–671.

WIGJ [Women's Initiatives for Gender Justice]. 2019. *The Hague Principles on Sexual Violence*. The Hague: Women's Initiatives for Gender Justice; https://thehagueprinciples.org

Wijngaards, John. 1995. 'Naked without Shame', *Mission Today* (Summer).

Williams, Craig A. 2010. *Roman Ideologies: Ideologies of Masculinity in Classical Antiquity*. Oxford: Oxford University Press, rev edn (first edn 1999).

Williams, Delores S. 1993. *Sisters in the Wilderness: The Challenge of Womanist God-Talk*. Maryknoll, NY: Orbis.

Williams, Joyce E. 1984. 'Secondary Victimization: Confronting Public Attitudes About Rape', *Victimology* 9: 66–81.

Williams, Joyce E., and Karen A. Holmes. 1981. *The Second Assault: Rape and Public Attitudes*. Westport, CT: Greenwood Press.

Winkler, Mathias. 2020. 'The Sexual Humiliation of Men: A Biblical Time Travel', *Shiloh Blog* (9 September); www.shilohproject.blog/the-sexual-humiliation-of-men-a-biblical-time-travel/

Zalewski, Marysia, Paula Drumond, Elisabeth Prügl, and Maria Stern, eds. 2018. *Sexual Violence Against Men in Global Politics*. New York: Routledge.

Zarkov, Dubravka. 2001. 'The Body of the Other Man: Sexual violence and the Construction of Masculinity, Sexuality and Ethnicity in Croatian Media', in Caroline O.N. Moser and Fiona C. Clark (eds.), *Victims, Perpetrators or Actors? Gender, Armed Conflict and Political Violence*. London and New York: Zed Books: 69–82.

Zeichmann, Christopher B. 2018. *The Roman Army and the New Testament*. Lanham, MD: Lexington Books/Fortress Academic.

Zugibe, Frederick T. 1989. 'Two Questions About Crucifixion', *Bible Review* 5 (2): 34–43.

Index

Note: Page numbers in *italics* indicate figures.

Abu Ghraib: naked prisoners at 8–11; sexual humiliation of prisoners 24; sexual violence against male detainees 29–30; sexual violence and humiliations of prisoners 31; stripping, enforced nudity and sexual abuse 21–22
Acts of Pilate 18
Adam and Eve, nudity and shame 12
Adb, Hayder Sabbar, prisoner in Abu Ghraib photo 9, 25n2
Afghanistan 10, 30
Alexander the Great 56
Alkimila 64n20
Allegra, Cécile 44
Ambrose of Milan 21
Amnesty International 4
anaskolopizein 64n28
anastauroun 64n28
Anjos, Márvio dos 66
Antiochus IV Epiphanes 25n6
Antiquities (Josephus), death of Herod Agrippa 38–39
Argentina 4; sexualised brutality in 30
Assyrian impalement, Roman crucifixion and 53–57
Augustine 26n16

Babylonian Empire 55
Bagram airbase: abuses at 10; stripping of Afghan captives at 30
beheading, execution by 20
Belser, Julia 33
Bible: abuse of Levite's wife 36–38; Good Samaritan 74; parable of judgement 74–75
Bible study 79–80n1; crucifixion of Jesus 71–72

Blackwell's Bookshop 2
Body of Jesus and Sexual Abuse, The (Trainor) 16
Bolsonaro, Michelle (First Lady) 67
Bosnia 4, 28
Boudicca, violation of daughters 33–34
Brazil 4; electrical shocks of Dragon's Chair 30
British Museum: Assyrian images in 54, 55; magical gem 50–51, *51*
Brownmiller, Susan 28
Bush administration, Abu Ghraib abuses 10

Celer (tribune), beheading of 20
Christian art: crucifixion in 18; loincloth in 18–19, 73–75
Christians 6; understanding of resurrection 6–7
Christology, Sobrino's 3
Christophobia 67, 68
Church Times (newspaper) 66
Cicero 31; on crucifixion 44–46
classrooms of hell, social media 7n4
Coleman, Kathleen 34
Cone, James 2, 3, 73
Constantine, abolishing crucifixion as punishment 18
Contextual Bible Study (CBS) 71
Cook, John Granger 53, 59, 60
Coponius Procurator of Judea 62n3
cross: as scandal or stumbling block 1; stripping of Jesus at 17–21; terminology of 47
Cross and the Lynching Tree, The (Cone) 73
cruces, term 57, 59

crucifixion 6, 78; accounts of Jesus' 49; artistic image of Jesus' 47; Assyrian impalement to Roman 53–57; Bible study of Jesus' 71–72; in Christian art 63n10; Christian art of Jesus' 47; Cicero on 44–46; the cross 44–53; historical development of Roman 43; infliction of shame 45; in New Testament 64n28; possibility of sexualised violence in Roman 42; Roman impalement 57–62; as sexualised violence 7n1; 'the stick' 44; term 56; terminology of Roman 53–54; of two men alongside Jesus 48–49
Crucifixion (Hengel) 53
crux 63n7; term 48, 49, 57, 65n31
crux commissa 47
crux compacta 62n7
crux decussata 62n7
crux immissa 47
crux simplex 63n14

Daldianus, Artemidorus 18
Dawson, Rosie 67
Democratic Republic of the Congo 70
Dialogue with Trypho (Justin) 61
Diodorus Siculus 56
Dionysius of Halicarnassus 18, 26n12
Dover, Kenneth 40n6
Dragon's Chair 30

Easter Saturday 77
El Salvador 4, 63n18; execution in 3–4; genital violence against women and men 30
Emmanuel, 'God is with us' 66, 68
enforced nudity 11; Abu Ghraib 21–22
England Lynndie (MP), sexual abuses at Abu Ghraib 9, 21–22
enhanced interrogation 10
execution, forms of 1

Figueroa, Rocío 76
Finney, Mark 12
flogging: Artemidorus Daldianus on 18; description of 25–26n10; full nudity at time of 52; of Jesus 16–17
Folha de Sao Paulo (newspaper) 66, 72

Gaddafi, Muammar: assault on 29, 35; authorising sexual violence 44
Gafney, Wil 73
Gaius Rabirius 45

Gavius 45
Geneva Conventions 10
Glimpse of Hell, A (Forrest) 5
GlobalPost 29
Global War on Terror 10
Goffman, Erving 69
Golgotha 1, 17, 48, 49, 54
Good Friday 77, 80n2
Good Samaritan, response to injured man 74
Gospel of John 79
Gospel of Nicodemus 18, 26n13
governor's palace 16; *see also praetorium*
Graystone, Andrew, on response of Good Samaritan 74
Greek culture, attitudes to nudity 13–14
Greenough, Christopher 24
Guantanamo, abuses at 10
Guardian, The (newspaper) 44
Guatemala 3, 4, 63n18
Gutiérrez, Gustavo 2

Hague Principles on Sexual Violence, stripping and enforced nudity 23
Harley-McGowan, Felicity 50, 51
Harman, Sabrina: Abu Ghraib experience 24; naked prisoner abuse 35; photos at Abu Ghraib 11; vulnerability of 'taxicab driver' prisoner 30–31
Harrison, Beverley 2
Hebrew Bible, attitudes to nudity in 12–13
Helena, Constantine's mother 18
Hellenised Jews 25n6
Hengel, Martin 53
Herman, Judith 77
Herod Agrippa 6, 28; death of 38–39
Herodotus 64n28
Herod the Great 38, 41n11
heterosexual, term 15
Heythrop College, London 3
Holmes, Karen 69
Homer's *Iliad* 14
homosexual, term 15

Iliad (Homer) 14
impalement 64n27; Assyrian 54–57
International Committee of the Red Cross, visit to Abu Ghraib 9
International Criminal Court 22
International Criminal Tribunal for former Yugoslavia (ICTY) 23, 40n1
International Criminal Tribunal for Rwanda (ICTR) 23

Iraqi prisoners: mistreatment at Abu Ghraib 6, 8; naked at Abu Ghraib 8–11; see also Abu Ghraib
Irenaeus (Bishop of Lyon) 48
irrumation 41n12

Jesus 7n1; accounts of crucifixion of 49; artistic re-covering of nakedness 73–74; Contextual Bible study of crucifixion of 71–72; Christian art of crucifixion 47–48; crucifixion in art 43, 73; dignity and recovery 72–75; flogging of 16; Justin Martyr on, as Paschal lamb 43–44, 61; King of the Jews 39; Mark and Matthew's accounts of mocking 34–35; Melito of Sardis on nakedness of 19; men crucified alongside 48–49; mistreatment by Jews 26n16; mocking of 5–6, 34–39, 68; nakedness in gospel texts 20; Paul on crucifixion of 49–50; as political prisoner 1; presence of women at crucifixion 49; resurrection of 75–78; sexualised violence 5; sexual violence in crucifixion of 68; stripping at the cross 17–21; strippings in *praetorium* 16–17; as victim of sexual abuse 66, 77–78
Jewish War (66–70 CE) 39; crucifixions during 46
Josephus: on Celer's beheading 20; crucifixion 44–45; crucifixion terms 64n28; death of Herod Agrippa 38–39; Jewish War 60; on Pilate 46; Varus (Governor of Syria) 46
Justin Martyr 57; crucifixion depiction 48; *Dialogue with Trypho* 45, 61; Jesus as Paschal lamb 43–44, 61; nails in Jesus' hands and feet 63n15

King of the Jews, Jesus 39
Knox, Robert 60
Kunarac Court 23

Lamentations, shame of nakedness 12
Latin Vulgate 54
Le Monde (periodical) 44
Le Roux, Elisabet 70–71
Levite's wife: rape and torture of 62n4; story of abuse of 36–38
liberation theology: Jesus' stripping in 8; Latin American 2
Libya 6, 44, 60
Lipsius, Justus 47, 65n33

loincloth, in Christian art 18–19, 73–75
Lorcians, unspeakable abuse against 32, 41n9
Lutheran Church 4
Luz, Ulrich 35

Mackie, Carolyn 24
magical gem, British Museum 50–51, *51*
male detainees, sexualised violence against 28–31
Marcellus 31
Medical Foundation for the Care of Victims of Torture 29
Melito of Sardis, on Christ's nakedness 19
#MeToo movement 68
Minucius Felix 52
mocking 27; of Jesus 5–6, 34–39; in praetorium 39–40; sexual violence and 27, 28; story of abuse of Levite's wife 36–38
Moral Essays (Seneca the Younger) 57
Moral Letters to Lucilius (Seneca the Younger) 57, 58

nakedness, term of uncovering 25n4; see also nudity
New Testament 54, 57, 64n28
Nicodemus, Gospel of 18, 26n13
Noah 12; nakedness in house 26n16; nakedness of 18; story of 12
nudity: attitudes in Hebrew Bible 12–13; attitudes in Roman Judaea 11–16; Greek attitudes to 13–14; Roman attitudes to 14–16; social meaning of 13

O'Collins, Gerald, on Jewish War 46
O'Donnell, Karen 68
Oneirocritica ('The Interpretation of Dreams'), Artemidorus Daldianus 18

Palatine graffito 18, 20, 26n14, 50, 51–52, 53, 62,73
Paschal lamb, Jesus as 43–44, 61
Pereire, Roger 50
Pereire gem 18, 26n14, 50–51, 52, 53, 60, 62, 73
Persian Empire 54, 56
Phileas Bishop of Thmuis, on outrage of Christian martyrs 20–21
Pieris, Aloysius 3
Pilate, Pontius 41n11, 46
pilegesh 41n13
Plancius, Gnaeus 31

Plato 40n7
Poole, Monica 77
Porciuncula, André 66
praetorium 5, 42; Jesus' suffering in 34–36; mockery of Jesus 48; mocking in 39–40; sexual assault in 27, 28; soldier abusing prisoners as 35–36; stripping in 5, 8, 27; strippings of Jesus in 16–17; whole cohort in 26n11
Prasutagus (King) 33
Principle of Mercy, The (Sobrino) 3
Punic Wars 56
Puteoli graffito 50, 52

Quirinius (Governor of Syria) 62n3

rape: during sacking of city 32; Roman captives 33; Sabine women in Rome (c. 750 BCE) 31; symbolism of 32
Reeder, Caryn, rape and sexual violence in war 32
Rembrandt, 'Crucifixion' painting 47
Republic, The (Plato) 40n7
resurrection: Christian understanding of 6–7; Jesus' experience 75–78
Roman Empire 11, 33; impalement 57–62; legend of rape of Sabine women 31; terminology for crucifixion 53–54
Romans: attitudes to nudity in Roman Judaea 11–16; bodies of subjected women in Roman art 33; concern for *dignitas* and *impudicita* 25n8; crucifixion and art 18; sexual protocol of 23; sexualised violence against captives 31–34; slaves punishment 45; stripping captives 15–16; torture in 34; treatment of Jews at crucifixion 20
Rwanda 4, 23, 28

Samuelsson, Gunnar 53, 60
Sánchez-Galan, Brenda 4
scandal, cross as 1, 7
Scarsella, Hilary 24
Second Assault, The (Williams and Holmes) 69
Second Punic War (218–201 BCE) 32
sedile, term 60
Seneca, the Younger 6, 40–41n8, 57–59
Sennacherib (Assyrian King) 55
sexual abuse 79; Abu Ghraib 21–22; blame and stigma 69–71; crucifixion as 2; Jesus as a victim of 5, 76; naked prisoner and 22

sexual assault, in *praetorium* 28
sexual crimes, International Criminal Court 22
sexual intercourse, uncovering nakedness 25n4
sexualised violence: crucifixion as 7n1; Jesus 68; possibility in Roman crucifixions 42; role of 1
sexual violence 2; against male detainees 28–31; against Roman captives 31–34; armed conflict and 4; issue of power and control 29; Jesus as victim of 77–78; Salvadoran conflict 4
shame, public nudity and 12–13
Sivakumaran, Sandesh, sexual violence 22
Smith, Mitzi 73
Smith, Shannel T. 76
Sobrino, Jon 7; Christology 3
social media, phrase 'classrooms of hell' 7n4
Society of Biblical Literature International Meeting 5
spoiled identity, stigma as 69
Sri Lanka 6, 29
state terror 5
stauros, term 53, 54, 55, 64n25, 65n31
'stick, the' 44
stigma, blame and of sexual abuse 69–71
stipes, term 57, 59
stipitem, term 48, 49, 57
stress positions, torture versus 10–11
stripping 11; Abu Ghraib 21–22; act of in mistreatment of Jesus 23–24; Afghan captives at Bagram air base 30; Jesus as sexual abuse 8, 16–21, 79; in *praetorium* 16–17, 27; stripping at cross 17–21
stumbling block, cross as 1, 75
suppendaeum 52
symposium 13, 25n7
Syria 6, 46, 62n3

Tacitus 7n1, 33, 46, 64n22
Tau cross 47
Tearfund 70
Tertullian 52; punishments in amphitheatre 34
Theology of Liberation, A (Gutiérrez) 2
Thiede, Barbara 25n5, 37–38
Tiberias 7n1

torture 78; stress positions versus 10–11; study of 5
Trainor, Michael 16, 24
tree of shame, crucifixion 45
Trible, Phyllis, on story of Levite's wife 36
Twitter 66, 67
Tzaferis, Vassilios 49

Ujamma Centre 71
UN Convention Against Torture 10
Union Seminary Quarterly Review 5
Union Theological Seminary 2, 3
University of KwaZulu-Natal 71
unspeakable violence 2, 6
US administration, stress positions *vs* torture 11
US military police (MP), naked Iraqi prisoners at Abu Ghraib 8–11

Varus (Governor of Syria), Josephus on 46
victim-blaming, stigma and 69–71
Walters, Jonathan 23
way of the cross 27
West, Cornel 2
West, Gerald 16
'wheel, the' 44
whole cohort, wording 26n11
Wigg-Stevenson, Natalie 2
Williams, Craig 15
Williams, Delores 73
Williams, Joyce 69
World War I 28
World War II 28

Yehohanan, victim of crucifixion 49

Zeichmann, Christopher 39

For Product Safety Concerns and Information please contact our EU
representative GPSR@taylorandfrancis.com
Taylor & Francis Verlag GmbH, Kaufingerstraße 24, 80331 München, Germany

www.ingramcontent.com/pod-product-compliance
Lightning Source LLC
Chambersburg PA
CBHW061959220426
43662CB00011B/1747